Assemblies for Primary Schools

Spring Term

Margaret Cooling

ASSOCIATION OF CHRISTIAN TEACHERS

RELIGIOUS AND MORAL EDUCATION PRESS

ASSEMBLIES FOR PRIMARY SCHOOLS: SPRING TERM

Religious and Moral Education Press
An imprint of Chansitor Publications Ltd,
a wholly owned subsidiary of Hymns Ancient & Modern Ltd of
St Mary's Works, St Mary's Plain
Norwich, Norfolk NR3 3BH

First published 1990
Reprinted 1991

ISBN 0 900274 60 3 spiral
0 900274 61 1 paperback

Printed in Great Britain by
BPCC Wheatons Ltd, Exeter

CONTENTS

Introduction   1
Practical Guidance   8

Group A: Love Is ...

1. Introductory assembly   14
2. Love makes ordinary people great (Love is the most important
    thing in life)   15
3. Love is patient (Enjoying today)   16
4. Love is kind (Love with its sleeves rolled up)   17
5. Love does not boast (Valuing other people)   18
6. Love is not rude (Tones of voice)   19
7. Love keeps no score of wrong (IOU)   20
8. Love does not rejoice in wrong (Clean washing)   21
9. Love is not proud (The pharisee and the tax collector)   22
10. Love is not jealous (Saul and David)   23
11. Love does not insist on its own way (How to get your own way)   24
12. Love puts up with a lot (The temper thermometer)   25
13. Love believes the best (The fox and the chickens)   26
14. Love lasts (Shelf life)   27
15. The big three (Faith, hope and love)   28
Follow-up Work for the Classroom   29

Group B: Trust and Obedience

1. Whom do you obey? (Obey the right person)   30
2. Facing difficult situations (David and Goliath)   31
3. Hearing is not enough (The two houses)   32
4. Trusting God when you don't feel brave (Gideon, superhero)   32
5. Trusting God for the unknown (Abraham)   34
6. Reluctant obedience (Jonah)   35
7. Obeying a simple command (Naaman)   36
8. Doing what is right (Daniel)   37
9. God with us (Three friends in the fire)   38
10. Keep trusting (Peter walking on the water)   39
Follow-up Work for the Classroom   39

Group C: Bible Stories

1. Not up to standard (Belshazzar's feast) — 40
2. The baby with a job to do (Moses) — 41
3. Invisible gifts (Solomon's choice) — 42
4. Super vision (David is chosen as king) — 43
5. Hope (The valley of dry bones) — 44

Follow-up Work for the Classroom — 45

Group D: Messages from the Prophets

1. What is a prophet? — 46
2. Pass the message on — 47
3. The plumb line (Amos) — 48
4. Baby reins (Hosea) — 49
5. The heart transplant (Ezekiel) — 50
6. Can a leopard change its spots? (Jeremiah) — 51
7. Drops in a bucket (Isaiah) — 52
8. The long arm (Isaiah) — 53
9. The river of justice (Amos) — 54
10. Ink stain (Isaiah) — 55

Follow-up Work for the Classroom — 55

Group E: Rules

1. Rules for life (The nature of rules) — 56
2. Negative rules — 57
3. Positive rules — 58
4. Breaking the rules (Psalm 53) — 59
5. Pictures of rules — 60

Follow-up Work for the Classroom — 60

Group F: Jesus's Job

1. Getting a Job (Jesus's job description) — 61
2. Spreading the good news (The patient farmer) — 63
3. Comforting the sad (What if …?) — 64
4. Giving sight to the blind (The blind man at Bethsaida) — 66
5. Setting the prisoners free (Invisible prisons) — 67
6. Making the lame walk (The man at the pool of Bethesda) — 68
7. Making the silent speak (Jesus heals a man unable to speak) — 69
8. Making the deaf hear (Jesus heals a deaf man) — 70
9. Healing the sick (A leprosy sufferer) — 71
10. Bringing the dead back to life (Jairus's daughter) — 72

Follow-up Work for the Classroom — 72

Group G: Lent and Holy Week

1. Lent 1 (Spring cleaning)   73
2. Lent 2 (Kukaras)   74
3. Shrove Tuesday (Forgiveness Tuesday)   75
4. Palm Sunday (Greetings)   76
5. Monday (Cheating)   77
6. Tuesday (Questions)   78
7. Wednesday (Giving)   79
8. Thursday (The servant king)   80
9. Good Friday (A sad day)   81
10. Easter Saturday (Waiting)   82
11. Easter Sunday (A joyful day)   83
12. The meaning of Easter (Reconciliation)   84
13. The meaning of Easter (Jesus the victor)   86
14. The meaning of Easter (New life)   87
15. The meaning of Easter (Remembering)   88

Follow-up Work for the Classroom   89

ACKNOWLEDGEMENTS

I would like to thank my husband Trevor for writing a substantial portion of the Introduction and for his help, support and advice in the writing of this book.

I would also like to thank Margaret Woodhall and Tracy Durnall for their help in checking the manuscript.

I am indebted to the primary schools of Stapleford who have experienced many of these assemblies, and our sons Robert and Terence on whom many of the ideas were tried out. I am also indebted to Arthur Rowe whose thinking was a source of inspiration.

My thanks also to my mother who not only contributed ideas but supported the whole family during the writing process.

Many of the ideas in this book were developed at Stapleford House, the Training Centre of the Association of Christian Teachers. Stapleford House regularly runs courses on assemblies and R.E. Further details can be obtained from: Stapleford House, Wesley Place, Stapleford, Nottingham NG9 8DP.

The story on p.26 is based on 'The Four Bulls' in *Themes for Assembly* by S. Brimer, published by Blackie.

The poem 'Whatif' on p.64 is reproduced by permission of Shel Silverstein and Jonathan Cape.

The song 'Oats, peas, beans and barley grow' on p.63 is published in *Singing and Dancing Games* by Macdonald Educational.

INTRODUCTION

The place of collective worship in the primary school has been firmly established by the 1988 Education Act. Each school now has to provide a minimum of 190 assemblies a year; a few schools may well have to organize over a thousand a year – no mean feat when it is considered that a good assembly can take over an hour to plan. This book is designed to help already overstretched primary teachers understand and fulfil their responsibilities in this area.

The Requirements of the 1988 Act

The Act lays down a number of requirements on school worship. These include:

1. There must be a *daily* act of worship for *all* pupils at the school and this should take place on the school's premises. This can be at any time of the day and does not have to be a gathering of the *whole* school together. A number of acts of worship can take place in any one school on any one day, as long as the pupils are in a normal teaching group or a group which exists for other school activities. A group cannot reflect the beliefs of a particular religious tradition; it is intended that any group shall comprise the normal mix of pupils found in the other educational activities of the school.

2. Parents may withdraw their children from acts of worship and teachers may also opt out of participating in them.

3. Most acts of worship in a term are to be 'wholly or mainly of a broadly Christian character'. An act of worship is considered to be of a broadly Christian character if it 'reflects the broad traditions of Christian belief without being distinctive of any particular Christian denomination'. The nature of other acts of worship which are not of a broadly Christian character is not defined in the Act.

4. In planning broadly Christian worship, schools are required to ensure that such acts are appropriate for their pupils, taking into account considerations of:
   - circumstances relating to the family background of the pupils concerned;
   - the ages and aptitudes of the pupils.

5. If headteachers feel that such broadly Christian worship is not appropriate for some or all of their pupils they can, after consulting with their governing body, apply to their local Standing Advisory Council on Religious Education for what is called a determination. This means that they can arrange other acts of worship, which are not of a broadly Christian character for some or all of their pupils. These acts may be distinctive of a particular religious *faith* but they cannot be distinctive of a particular religious *denomination*. This is a distinction which may, in some cases, require considerable theological expertise to discern.

6. The responsibility for worship arrangements lies with the headteacher after consultation with the governing body.

The arrangements for Church and other voluntary schools are slightly different. In these cases the character of the worship will be in accordance with their original foundation and the final responsibility for the arrangements rests with the governing body, after consultation with the headteacher.

The challenge for teachers is how to implement these requirements in a professional manner. What follows will I hope give some guidelines in charting a way through a complex maze.

The Problems

The requirements for Christian worship have been criticized in some quarters as Christian imperialism. John Hull in an editorial in the *British Journal of Religious Education* saw great danger in 'the tribalistic and protective emotions which have been aroused by a partisan Christian faith'. The Muslim Educational Trust issued a pamphlet early in 1989 saying Muslim children will be required 'to pray to Jesus as the Son of God, learn about the Trinity and thus commit the awesome sin of Shirk, associating others with Allah. This is the worst thing a Muslim can do.' They have therefore advised Muslim parents to withdraw their children from school worship. Teachers will need to be very aware of the pain that can be caused to parents by the requirement that worship be broadly Christian.

The second problem is both practical and ethical. Clearly children cannot be compelled to worship. Bitter experience of 600 children refusing to sing a hymn in an Easter service convinced me of that very early in my teaching career. Even if worship could be compelled it certainly should *not* be. Just because infants can be made unquestioningly to pray to Jesus does not mean that such activity is legitimate.

However, despite the problems associated with worship, educationally we cannot do without it. There are two reasons why this is the case.

Firstly, the research by the Religious Experience Research Unit at Oxford and Nottingham Universities indicates that childhood experience of stillness, peace, awe, wonder, mystery, celebration, reverence and belonging are of central importance in promoting spiritual development. In a school day, and indeed in most children's lives, school worship will be one of the few contexts where such experiences can be explored and reflected upon.

Secondly, religious beliefs and practices may appear simply as odd people doing and believing odd things unless there is some experiential understanding of what belief means to the believer. Without school worship there will be little opportunity to give children the 'feels that make the tolds fall into place' in the religious realm. It could be argued that it provides a unique opportunity to help children become more aware of the importance of the human search for meaning in the face of life's mysteries.

Planning worship is rather like being asked to plot a course through a minefield. There will be mishaps on the way and it will no doubt be a hair-raising experience, but the satisfaction and rewards of reaching the other side are enormous. Successful school worship can provide some of those special moments for both teachers and pupils.

Some Ways through the Minefield

In order to make a success of school worship I would suggest that the following principles are adopted.

(a) Distinguish between assembly and worship

For years we have been used to conflating these two activities and school worship has been equated with any act of gathering together of the school. The problem of worship has in this way been ducked. The Department of Education and Science circular 3/89 on school worship makes it quite plain that these two activities are distinct. Teachers are bound by contract to attend assembly; however, they have the right to opt out of worship.

The gathering of the school community in an assembly is educationally an important activity, but it does not have to take place every day. Worship does, however, have to be a daily act. In these notes I shall ignore the question of assembly, my comments are addressed solely to the activity of *worship*. I shall still use the word assembly to describe the act of worship, since this is the word most commonly used by teachers. Its specific and particular sense in this book should, however, always be remembered. Even if the two activities cannot be physically separated, the teacher should have a clear understanding of their distinct functions.

(b) Be aware of the dangers

One important way of avoiding mines is to be aware of their presence in advance. There are five that are the most frequent causes of explosion in school worship.

(i) Compromising pupil integrity

This is what Muslim parents quite rightly object to. Christian parents are equally incensed when their children are invited to make offerings to a Hindu goddess in the name of multiculturalism. Many parents who are not religious themselves are deeply offended when schools assume that their children will, for example, pray to Jesus. The sensitivities of parents vary enormously in this respect, but it is quite wrong for schools to expect them to bury their deepest convictions for the sake of some educational ideal. Children should not be required to compromise their integrity through involvement in acts of school worship.

(ii) *Misrepresenting religious faith*
This is another cause of offence to religious communities. The two most common manifestations in school are syncretism and relativism. Syncretism is when an attempt is made to unify different religions. Relativism is when religions are treated as culturally specific – for example, when it is implied that Islam is true for Arabs whereas Christianity is true for Westerners. Schools have fallen into both of these traps in their attempts to produce non-divisive, multicultural acts of worship. It is a mistake, however, to think that a sense of community can be fostered by arranging acts of worship that may turn out to be offensive to particular religious minorities.

This is not to say that syncretism or relativism are wrong, indeed they are positions taken by some religions. What is wrong is for schools to assume they are the only valid position. It is equally a mistake, although a less common practice, for schools to imply that all genuine religions are exclusive, claiming to be the only way to God. This whole area is very complex and teachers should be wary of thinking that they can resolve the theological issues involved on educational grounds.

(iii) *Messages from reluctant staff*
Most teachers can remember assemblies from their own school days which were led by teachers who clearly didn't believe in what they were doing. These memories should be enough to ensure that we never put fellow teachers in the position of leading worship when they feel compromised by such an act. Particular care over this will need to be exercised by schools which arrange for worship to take place in class or form groups.

(iv) *Trivializing the spiritual*
Many adults will also have memories of being harangued by the headteacher about graffiti in the toilets or litter on the field, just after having sung a hymn about the love of God. To imply, by association, that God is on the side of school rules or that He cares ultimately about the success of the football or netball team is to trivialize the spiritual realm. This is one very good reason for having a clear separation in teachers' minds between assembly and worship. It may be a very good reason for physically separating the two events.

(v) *Organizing inappropriate worship*
The Act is quite clear that worship must be appropriate for the very mixed population of children present in most schools in Britain. All schools will have minorities of pupils belonging to families who are active members of faith communities. The vast majority of pupils will come from homes which are largely secularized. This makes the 'congregation' very different from that in church. The challenge of providing appropriate worship for children from secularized backgrounds is very different from that facing any Christian minister or Sunday School leader. If failure or large numbers of

withdrawals are to be avoided, schools will have to think in very different terms from those employed by people organizing worship in the Christian community. School and church are not the same. That is why the Act refers to collective worship as opposed to corporate worship. The latter is an activity that can take place only amongst people who have shared religious beliefs.

(c) *Think carefully about the meaning of worship*

Worship is usually seen as adoration of God by a group of believers who are in voluntary association. Such a view makes it a totally inappropriate activity for a school whose members are compelled to be there and who represent a variety of different faith positions. Unless we can produce a broader understanding of worship it has little future as a school-based activity. No amount of legal compulsion will overcome the ethical and religious objections.

In fact even amongst a group of committed believers, a wide variety of *responses* will be in evidence during any one act of worship. The range of these is illustrated in the list below, which is by no means exhaustive:

- awareness of
- appreciation of
- respect for
- preference for
- commitment to
- devotion to
- adoration of.

This diversity of response indicates a way forward for worship in schools. Worship is offensive only if pupils are compelled to respond in a particular way. If acts of worship can be designed which leave pupils free to respond in any of the seven ways listed above, then the main problem of compulsory worship is overcome. One of the chief questions in the minds of those planning acts of worship should therefore be whether this activity leaves pupils free to respond in a way that is appropriate for them or whether it compels and expects one type of response only. The former should always be the case. No presumptions should be made on behalf of pupils.

Another way forward is to consider exactly what *activities* are associated with worship. Traditionally prayer, hymn singing and readings from sacred texts have been seen to characterize worship. Again I would argue that this is an unnecessarily narrow conception. A number of other activities can legitimately be called worship. Amongst these are:

- reflection on the meaning and purpose of life
- pondering ultimate questions
- developing a sense of transcendence
- responding to challenge
- experiential exploration of a religious idea
- celebration of learning about religion
- learning from the experience of others.

All these are legitimate educational activities, and when combined with an approach which gives freedom of pupil response, they present a very positive formula for thinking about school worship.

Practically, what has been said in this section amounts to two priorities for the teacher.

(i) Consideration should be given to the language that is used when conducting worship. Inclusive language such as 'we believe that' or 'we will all pray' should be avoided in favour of language that grounds beliefs in a particular faith tradition. To return to the Muslim concern mentioned earlier, it is quite wrong to say that Jesus is the Son of God, but legitimate to ask children to reflect on *the Christian belief* that Jesus is the Son of God. The former insists on assent, the latter presents a belief which the children are free to respond to in their own way, even if that response only amounts to an awareness that this belief is important to Christians.

(ii) Consideration should also be given to allowing pupils to function comfortably in worship secure in a sense of their own religious identity. For younger pupils this will be derived from their family, for older ones it will be much more a matter of their own personal conviction. Worship should be so structured that each pupil can be happy either with the notion that this activity is an adventure into something that he or she identifies with or alternatively that it is an exploration into something that is 'not me'. Here exploration does not imply assent. Respecting pupil identity should be of paramount importance in preparing worship and the demands will be different depending on the type of school and the nature of the community it serves.

(d) *Making worship 'broadly Christian'*
This particular phraseology has been hedged about with several qualifiers. What exactly is meant by this is as yet unclear and can be definitively determined only by the law courts. Even 'experts' in R.E. cannot decide what is meant. Thus John Hull, Reader in Religious Education at Birmingham University, has argued that Christian collective worship is optional for schools, whereas George Oliver, a former Inspector for Religious Education in the Inner London Education Authority, asserts that the majority of acts of worship in a school over a term must be Christian. If such people cannot agree there seems little hope of a definitive definition being available for the chalkface practitioner. There are, however, three things that are very clear from the Act.

First, broadly Christian worship in schools is not the same as distinctively or uniquely Christian worship. The Secretary of State for Education has stated that such an act of worship can include material drawn from non-Christian, and even non-religious, traditions provided that, taken as a whole, it reflects the traditions of Christian belief.

Secondly, broadly Christian worship has to reflect the broad traditions of Christian *belief*, not the broad traditions of Christian *worship*. This is a significant statement because the word 'belief' is not the one that would most readily spring to mind when framing such a clause. School worship is to be a communal exploration of beliefs in a manner appropriate for schoolchildren and not a kaleidoscope of the practices of Christian adults from a variety of church backgrounds. However, this is not to imply that school worship should consist of monologues on particular doctrines! Experiential approaches are essential and it is most important to stimulate the affective as well as the cognitive. So, for example, in an assembly on creation, children should come to feel awe and wonder and not just be told about it.

Thirdly, worship will *reflect* the broad traditions of Christian belief. It is not required that these beliefs be systematically expounded or affirmed or even that they form the central focus of the act of worship. It is only necessary that they be reflected in what happens.

I would suggest that there are two understandings of the phrase 'broadly Christian' which can be profitably developed:

(i) There are many values and beliefs which are part of the broad traditions of Christian belief but which are also widely held in society at large. Examples include a sense of awe at the natural world and the merits of sacrificial love. Such values can be explored and celebrated in school worship in a manner that complements the way they are taught in the classroom and communicated through the ethos of the school.

(ii) There are various concepts which are central to traditional Christian belief. Examples include reconciliation, incarnation and creation. Such beliefs are shared across Christian traditions and can therefore legitimately form a focus for school worship, as long as what we have already said about freedom of pupil response is kept clearly in mind.

Conclusion

The function of this book is to help the busy primary school teacher fulfil the major requirements of the 1988 Education Act in relation to school worship. The acts of worship in the book are designed to be appropriate to primary age children, using the children's experience to explore Christian belief. They are either of a *wholly* or of a *mainly* broadly Christian character and the teacher will have to decide which can be used in the particular context of his or her school. Some of the material may be felt to be appropriate only in church schools, but the vast majority of it can be used in most schools as long as the teachers are sensitive to the needs and background of their children. Follow-up work is suggested so that worship and classroom work can be integrated.

Our hope is that teachers will be able to use these ideas to organize acts of worship which enable children to learn from Christian belief in a way that promotes their spiritual, moral, cultural and mental development.

PRACTICAL GUIDANCE

In the Introduction to this book I have examined the legal and educational context in which school worship takes place. In this section I shall suggest a series of 'dos and don'ts' to which teachers and others can refer in the planning of school worship. Individual teachers may wish to add guidelines of their own. This is followed by some practical guidance on the use of this book.

Dos and Don'ts

There are various pitfalls to be avoided when taking assemblies. Below are a few suggestions of things to beware of.

Dos and don'ts for teachers taking Christian assemblies

1. Avoid tying religious faith with the children's behaviour too tightly. Of course there is a close connection between faith and action but faith should never be used to manipulate. Children rightly resent such attempts. Religious faith should be seen as something that changes both the child's and the adult's behaviour. Religious faith should not be used to bolster school rules.

Example: Good Christians do not run in the corridor or drop litter.

2. Do not put people in a corner. Both adults and children need to feel that their identity is protected. Use a non-offensive phrase such as 'Christians believe' or 'Jesus said'. Do not say 'You should…' or 'We all…'. The use of non-offensive phrases allows people emotionally to opt in or to opt out of an assembly. It allows people to decide their attitude to an assembly and either identify with the faith being explored or explore that faith from a greater distance. With very young children there is obviously a difficulty of understanding such phrases, but even so safeguards need building in.

3. Do speak to their world. Even in the short space of an assembly the rule of starting where the children are and finishing where they are not still applies. Start from the known to lead children to the unknown. Move from the familiar to the unfamiliar.

Example: A simple transformer or the use of the dressing-up box can start a child thinking about changes. You can then lead them on to thinking about changing on the inside.

4. Don't make comments about others faiths, agnostics or atheists.

5. Don't go into highly controversial areas. Assembly is not the place for controversy. No one can disagree with you if you are taking the assembly and the rest of the staff might feel you are abusing your platform.

6. Don't be denominational. The law allows you to be Christian but not denominational in an act of worship. It is better for the children if Christians share their agreements rather than dwell on their differences.

7. Be aware of the dangers of raising areas of pastoral concern unless you have been specifically asked to do so. Such areas need careful preparation and follow-up by all the staff. Subjects such as war, death, divorce and similar matters are generally better dealt with in a pastoral situation.

8. Don't make casual allusions that are not followed up. Asides confuse children. Stick very strictly to the subject and do not deviate from it.

9. Assemblies are very short and children understand things better if they come in small parcels. Choose one small area and deal with it well rather than ranging over a large subject.

10. Do not make children pray, instead ask them to listen while you pray or read a prayer. An acceptable formula might be something like this:
> 'I am going to pray (or read a Christian prayer). I would like you to keep very still, close your eyes and listen carefully to the words. Those of you who wish to can join in with the Amen (I agree) at the end.'

In this way children are not joining in Christian prayers against their will, but they are listening respectfully and possibly thinking about the prayer.

11. If you use hymns and songs remember to think carefully about the words, in the light of some of the dangers of worship already described. For example, singing the song 'Jesus is Lord' would be inappropriate in many situations.

Dos and don'ts for visitors taking Christian assemblies

All the dos and don'ts for teachers apply to visitors but there are some extra ones which are also relevant.

1. Do be friendly and polite. This should go without saying. Thank the school for inviting you and treat both the staff and pupils with respect.

2. Do realize you are a guest and probably not there by right. There should be no attitude of infiltrating enemy territory! Visitors serve the school as part of the community and *vice versa*. Visitor participation in assemblies should be seen as a learning partnership on both sides. Both should be open to criticism and praise. The school should be able to cope with the occasional disaster and help the visitor to learn from their mistakes. The visitor must be open to such positive criticism.

3. Accept a healthy suspicion on the part of the school. This is part of their pastoral role, appreciate the fact that they do not let just anybody in to take assemblies. Offer references if necessary, someone who knows how you

relate to children. Offer to let the headteacher see what you are going to say beforehand if he or she wishes to.

4. Do remember that the children do not volunteer for assembly. You can help them explore Christianity but do not 'push' faith in an inappropriate way.

5. Remember it is a school not a church; do not assume belief or familiarity with Christianity or biblical stories.

6. Do bear in mind the Christian members of staff. You can either be a great encouragement to them or make life difficult. Remember it is they who will hear the comments in the staffroom.

7. Make sure you manage the practical details well. Organize the time, date, venue and duration of the assembly. Make sure you know the age group of the children you are talking to. Telephone the school a day or so beforehand to reassure them that you are coming and to make any necessary arrangements.

8. Do make visual aids and writing large enough to be seen from the back. Small pictures, tiny writing and small objects will cause the children to start kneeling up to see and they will soon lose interest in what they cannot see.

9. Do not undermine the school in the remarks that you make.

Example: We all know how horrible school dinners are.

10. Don't make sexist or racist comments. Take the same care over your language as teachers do. Ask girls to help as well as boys. Encourage girls as well as boys to answer questions. Are all your main characters white and male or are some of them girls or black or handicapped?

11. Remember that sight reading is an adult skill. If you are going to teach the children a song or have something for them to read, do help them. Fluency in reading does not come until the middle junior years and for some it comes much later. Read things with children. Always print in lower case letters, never capitals.

NOTE: Detailed guidance on visitors taking Christian assemblies can be found in the books *Your Turn to Take Assembly* by Howard Cunnington, published by ACT (available from ACT, 2 Romeland Hill, St Albans, Herts. AL3 4ET) and *Leading School Worship* by Janet King, published by Monarch.

Dos and don'ts for the school that invites visitors in to take assembly

1. Do be polite and helpful. Many teachers are so busy that visitors are sometimes left feeling abandoned. Make sure they have the equipment and information they need.

2. Do arrange for someone to meet a visitor. It is very unnerving to walk into a school and not be able to find the head or secretary.

3. Do introduce and thank a visitor.

4. Do brief a visitor well. They need to know the situation they are coming into and what you are happy for them to do.

5. Do check visitors. Not all visitors are suitable for taking assemblies.

6. Do phone the visitor beforehand to confirm that they are coming.

7. If your school sings hymns do give the visitor a hymn book. They can feel very silly standing silently in front of three hundred singing children.

8. Be positive in your criticism, but be honest. Be prepared for the occasional disaster, but treat it as a joint learning experience.

Using the Material

This book is concerned with leading Christian assemblies, but tries to recognize the stress that such assemblies can put on staff. The following features have therefore been included:

Seventy assemblies

There are seventy assemblies in this book, which approximately reflects the length of the spring term. A school can choose what percentage of Christian assemblies they wish to use from this collection to contribute towards the Christian input into their assembly programme.

School weeks

The assemblies are blocked largely in groups of five, ten, fifteen and twenty so that they fit in with a five-day school week pattern.

Longer themes

The assemblies are blocked in themes so that one theme covers a whole week, fortnight or month. This allows teachers to explore an idea in depth rather than doing a variety of 'one offs'.

Active assemblies

As far as possible the assemblies involve the children in active exploration of their own experience. Normal classroom practice is carried over into assemblies so that teachers can use familiar techniques with the children who are encouraged to join in. Because the assemblies involve interaction with the children every word of an assembly cannot be written out. Suitable questions are indicated, but obviously the way the conversation develops depends on the pupils' contribution.

A variety of material

All the assemblies are broadly Christian but some deal with issues that are more centrally Christian than others. This variety is provided to allow as many teachers as possible to take part without feeling that their own position is compromised. Some teachers, for example, might be happy taking an assembly on the Good Samaritan but would be uncomfortable taking an assembly on Easter.

A variety of methods

These assemblies use a variety of methods: drama, storytelling, games and art. Teachers can select from the assemblies the type of material they feel confident in handling.

Preparation

We recognize the pressures on teachers and have tried to keep preparation down to the minimum. Most of what would be called preparation is actually done in the assembly 'Blue Peter' style so that you do not have to have things ready prepared. To save further time we recommend that an 'Assembly Box' be kept in the staff room with most of the basic materials you will need to execute these assemblies.

The Assembly Box

This is a storage box (a cardboard box will do) that contains basic materials such as card, paper and pens. The contents should be checked regularly against a list stuck to the outside. If possible appoint an older child to check the box once a week.

Other items which are needed for a particular assembly can be brought in by the teacher or the pupils. Wherever possible delegate what preparation there is by asking a child or an adult helper to make sure that you have in the box what you need for your specific assembly by checking the 'You will need' section of the assembly against the contents of the assembly box.

Contents of the assembly box:

1. Pritt stick
2. Sugar paper
3. A4 paper
4. Large sheets of paper (lining paper or the back of wallpaper will do)
5. Scissors
6. Card (offcuts left over from art classes and some A4)
7. Blu-Tak
8. Several balls of coloured wool
9. Felt pens, large and small
10. If you use an overhead projector (OHP), acetates and pens will be needed.

Health and safety

All paints and glues used should be non-toxic. Any scissors used should be the safe variety normally used in primary schools. If you decide to light any candles this should be done only by an adult with due regard to safety and they should be blown out so that any decorations or greenery are not ignited. All activities should be carried out with a normal regard for safety.

Language

The language of the assemblies has been kept as simple as possible, but infant/nursery teachers might feel they need to adapt the language further.

Passages from the Bible have been paraphrased or adapted. Although they are true to the message or meaning of a passage, they are not a direct or literal translation.

Prayer

The prayers included are short and broadly Christian. They are deliberately short in order to help those staff who do not feel comfortable saying prayers. If a member of staff is happy to say prayers they can always extend them themselves.

Follow-up work

A small amount of follow-up work is provided at the end of each group of assemblies so that ideas stimulated in assembly can be followed up in the classroom in greater depth.

A 1. Introductory Assembly

You will need:

Card/paper, scissors, pens, Blu-Tak.

Introductory activity

Have fourteen hearts drawn on pieces of card or paper, about the size of a saucer. Ask children to come out and help you cut them out. Alternatively, have the hearts already cut out, with the word 'Love …' written on them. You can be cutting out a large heart from sugar paper. It needs to be large enough to take all fourteen small hearts, though some can be displayed around it as well as inside it.

Write the words 'LOVE IS …' on the large heart and Blu-Tak it to the wall.

Ask the children to Blu-Tak the little hearts around it and inside it.

Talk

Ask the children what they think love is.

Love is one of those words that can mean very many different things.

In other languages there are often many words for love, but we have only one. This one word 'love' has many meanings. What do the following examples mean?

I *love* chocolate.   I *love* Dr Who.
My parents *love* me.   I *love* going swimming.

Write out each of these sentences then try to rewrite them with the children without using the word 'love'. Alternatively, ask the children for their own examples and then try to rewrite them.

Example: I am a fan of Dr Who.

For the next two weeks we shall be looking at how the Bible describes love.

Each day we shall add something to one of the small hearts until we have many descriptions of love.

Comment

The word love has so many meanings that it is like a parcel with many layers of wrapping paper – the type you use for 'pass the parcel'. Each day we shall unpack a little more of the meaning of this word love.

Note for teachers: You may wish to write the descriptions of love on pieces of paper and put them between layers of wrapping paper to make a parcel, as sweets are put between each layer for 'pass the parcel'. One layer can be taken off each day.

Prayer

May we be more loving in what we say, in what we do and in what we think about others.

A 2. Love Makes Ordinary People Great

You will need:

Paper, pen and Blu-Tak.

Introductory activity

Draw a simple version of Superman/woman on the paper and ask what makes them great. Is it money, brains, looks, bravery, superpowers or skill?

Talk

Saint Paul wrote about what really makes people special. You don't have to be superman or superwoman. Paul said love makes ordinary people great.

This is what he said:

If I can speak every language in heaven and on earth but have no love, I am a like a noisy gong or a clanging bell. If I am really brainy and understand everything in the universe but have no love, I am nothing. If I can do miracles and great deeds of bravery but have no love, it does me no good at all.

Take down the first heart and complete the sentence so that it reads: 'Love … makes people great'. Blu-Tak it inside the large heart.

Comment

Christians believe that you do not need any qualifications for love except a loving heart. You do not have to be wealthy or brainy or brave, just loving.

Prayer

Thank you, Father, that Love is one skill that everyone can develop. Help us to put it into practice.

A 3. Love Is Patient

You will need:

A pen, Blu-Tak, a large sheet of paper, felt-tip pen.

Introductory activity

Take down the next heart and complete the sentence so that it reads: 'Love ... is patient'. Blu-Tak it inside the large heart.

Ask the children what they think the word patient means.

Talk

Draw a series of large speech bubbles. Under them write the words 'baby', 'child', 'teenager', 'adult' and ask the children what each of these 'can't wait' for. Here are some examples:

Comment

Patience is enjoying today and not wasting the time you have because you always want to rush on to the next thing. Love is also patient with other people, not trying to rush them on to the next thing. Love lets people go at their own pace.

Prayer

Thank you for all the time you give us. May we enjoy all of it and not wish our time away.

A 4. Love Is Kind

You will need:

A pen, Blu-Tak.

Introductory activity

Take down the next heart and complete the sentence so that it reads: 'Love … is kind'. Blu-Tak it inside the large heart.

Ask the children what they think kindness is.

Talk

Christians call kindness 'Love in action'. Kindness is very practical, it is love with its sleeves rolled up and its boots on, getting on with the job of helping others.

Draw a cartoon of kindness; use the one below if you need to.

Comment

Why do you think that in this cartoon kindness has its sleeves rolled up? What sort of job would you roll up your sleeves for? Why do you think it has boots on? What jobs would you put on your wellington boots for?

Prayer

Help us to put love into action in the form of kindness to show others that we care.

A 5. *Love Does Not Boast*

Love...
does not
boast

You will need:

A pen, paper (optional), Blu-Tak.

Introductory activity

Take down the next heart and complete the sentence so that it reads 'Love ... does not boast'. Blu-Tak it inside the large heart.

Ask the children for some examples of boasting. Write some of them down if you wish.

Explain that boasting is when one person tries to make themselves look big by saying that they are better, richer, cleverer or prettier than other people.

Talk

Paul was one of the early Christians, he used to travel around different countries telling people about Jesus. Wherever he went he started new churches and looked after the new Christians.

Some people in one of the new churches were boasting that they were better than Paul and telling people not to listen to him. Paul replied by doing a little boasting himself just to show how silly it is. Here is what he said.

I come from a very proud family; I am one of the great, great grandchildren of Abraham. I have worked harder than anyone else to serve Christ. I have been in prison many times. I have been beaten and left for dead and I have been whipped many times, both with a lash and with a rod. Once stones were thrown at me. I have been shipwrecked three times, once spending a day and a night in the sea. I have been in danger from rivers, bandits and people who were determined to stop me. I often went without sleep and knew cold, hunger and thirst. I once had to escape from a city by being lowered over the walls in a basket because the king was going to arrest me. Every day I have all the problems of the churches I look after.

To boast like this is stupid, it only makes me look a fool. People will not think more of me if I boast. If I must boast, I will boast of the things I *cannot* do because then people will see how great God is when good things happen. They will know that God has done them and not think it was me!

(Adapted from 2 Corinthians 11 and 12)

Comment

Boasting is very unpleasant, it makes the person who is boasting look silly. It is also very hurtful and often untrue.

Prayer

Teach us, Lord, to value other people and help us not to make them feel small by our boasting.

A 6. Love Is Not Rude

Love . . .
is not
rude

You will need:

A pen, Blu-Tak.

Introductory activity

Take down the next heart and complete the sentence so that it reads: 'Love … is not rude'. Blu-Tak it inside the large heart.

Talk

People can be rude in many ways: in what they say, in the way they say things and in what they do.

Most people know when they are doing or saying something rude, but some people have difficulty working out whether they have said something in a rude way.

Listen to these words and see if you can notice any difference in the way I say them.

Thanks.   *Thanks!*

A drink of orange, please.   *A drink of orange, please.*

That's really great.   *That's really great!*

That's cheered me up a lot.   *That's cheered me up a lot!*

(Add your own examples.)

Even the word 'please' can be said so that it sounds more like an order than a request.

Comment

The Bible says the way we talk to people can either be loving or not. How we speak can either help or hurt. The way we say things matters as much as what we say.

Prayer

Father, may we accept all people as precious and valuable and show that we think they are worthy by the way we treat them and how we speak.

A 7. *Love Keeps No Score of Wrong*

Love . . .
keeps no
score of
wrong

You will need:

A pen, paper, some money, Blu-Tak.

Introductory activity

Take down the next heart and complete the sentence so that it reads: 'Love … keeps no score of wrong'. Blu-Tak it inside the large heart.

Let a few children borrow some money and write them a large IOU on A4 paper. Explain that the IOU is your record of what they owe. When you want the money back you will give them the IOU and you will have the money back. Write IOU at the top of another piece of paper and write down the sort of debts people keep a record of. This is an example.

IOU

One kick
One punch
Two pinches

Talk

Pupils are always coming to teachers and parents and saying, 'He hit me first,' or 'She deserved it, I owed her a kick for what she did to me.'

People keep a record of wrongs, like an IOU, and sometimes demand payment by doing back to other people what they did to them.

In the Bible Paul said that love does not keep a record of wrong. Love tears up the IOU. [Tear up the ones you wrote.] Love forgives.

Comment

Keeping a score or record of wrongs is sometimes called 'bearing a grudge'. It is a refusal to forgive. We could rewrite Paul's description of love and say, 'Love does not bear a grudge.'

Prayer

Teach us to forgive the wrongs done to us and not to keep a record of them.

A 8. Love Does Not Rejoice in Wrong

Love . . .
does not
rejoice in
wrong

You will need:

A pen, Blu-Tak.

Some washing: one piece clean, one piece grubby and one piece really dirty. You can do this by using three white hankies and deliberately 'dirtying' them with very dilute powder paint.

Introductory activity

Take down the next heart and complete the sentence so that it reads: 'Love ... does not rejoice in wrong'. Blu-Tak it inside the large heart.

Explain that 'rejoice' means 'to be very happy'.

Ask the children to compare the pieces of washing and put them in order of cleanliness.

Talk

Sometimes when one person gets in trouble other people enjoy it. Some people stand around and watch if there is a fight or just like to see other people doing things they shouldn't be doing. One of the reasons for this is that if they see someone else do wrong it makes them feel better.

Just as a very clean piece of washing makes the other pieces look dirty, so a very good person sometimes annoys others because they show up others' bad behaviour. For this reason some people like it when someone else is bad; it makes them feel less bad, just as the grubby piece of washing looks grey compared with the clean piece but quite good compared with the really dirty piece of washing.

Comment

When people get into trouble for doing something wrong, they often say things such as 'Everybody does it' or 'She made more mess than I did'. This is one of the reasons why some people are happy when others do something wrong, they can point to the others' behaviour to excuse their own. 'Love,' said Paul, 'is happy when people do what is right.'

Prayer

Help us, Father, to be sorry when other people get into trouble and not to enjoy it. Help us to imagine what it is like and how we would like people to behave towards us.

A 9. Love Is Not Proud

Love . . .
is not
proud

You will need:

A pen, Blu-Tak.

Introductory activity

Take down the next heart and complete the sentence so that it reads: 'Love … is not proud'. Blu-Tak it inside the large heart.

Ask the children for descriptions of pride.

Here is a poem about pride.

They say my reading's wonderful,
My maths's beyond compare.
I know my art is very good,
And my writing's more than fair.

At P.E. I'm a whizz kid,
At most sports I excel,
At music I beat all the rest,
In topics I do well.

I'm beautiful and charming,
I'm graceful through and through.
I'm glad that I am like I am,
It must be awful being you!

Talk

Here is a story Jesus told about pride.

In one of his stories Jesus paints the picture of two men who went into the Temple to pray. One was a pharisee, a religious leader, respected by all the people, the other was a hated tax collector despised by everyone. The pharisee stood up before God, feeling very proud of himself, and said, 'I thank you God that I am not like other men, not like that horrible tax collector over there.' The tax collector was quite different, he was so sorry for the wrong he had done he knelt before God and asked God to forgive him. Jesus said it was the tax collector who was the better person in God's eyes. People should not be puffed up with their own importance.

Comment

There are two types of pride: there is a right sort when people are proud of something they have made or done and there is a wrong sort when people think they are better than anyone else. People who are proud often boast about what they can do and make others feel small or useless.

Prayer

Give us the right sort of pride, Lord, that will enjoy being able to use the gifts you have given us without boasting and hurting others.

A 10. Love Is Not Jealous

Love . . .
is not
jealous

You will need:

A pen, Blu-Tak.

Introductory activity

Take down the next heart and complete the sentence so that it reads: 'Love … is not jealous'. Blu-Tak it inside the large heart.

Ask the children what jealousy is.

Talk

Here is a story from the Bible.

Saul was king of Israel, and David was a young soldier in his army. David was a very good fighter and when he came back from the wars people danced through the streets, saying what a good soldier he was. Saul became extremely jealous; the more he thought about David, the more he hated him even though David had done nothing wrong. Saul became so angry with David for being a better soldier than he was that his anger got the better of him and he threw his spear at David, trying to pin him to the wall. David ducked but he knew he was no longer safe. Back in his home David told his wife Michal what had happened. Michal realized that Saul would not rest until he had captured David so she helped him escape and placed a statue in his bed so that it would look as if David was in bed asleep.

   Some time later the soldiers came to arrest David. Michal protested, saying David was ill, but the soldiers had orders to fetch him even if he was sick in bed. The soldiers went to the bed and discovered that it was only a statue lying there. They reported it to Saul. When Saul found he had been tricked and David had escaped he was furious and his jealousy led him to hunt David for many years.

Comment

Saul was jealous and it eventually led to him trying to kill David. This was an extreme case, but jealousy often leads to arguments and broken friendships. Not being jealous is being able to say to someone, 'That's a nice dress' or 'That's a good game' without wishing it was yours instead of your friend's.

Prayer

Help us, Father, to enjoy other people's talents and possessions without wishing they were ours instead.

A 11. Love Does Not Insist on Its Own Way

Love . . . does not insist on its own way

You will need:

A pen, Blu-Tak, a large sheet of paper, felt-tip pen.

Introductory activity

Take down the next heart and complete the sentence so that it reads: 'Love ... does not insist on its own way'. Blu-Tak it inside the large heart.

Ask the children to say what 'wanting your own way' means. Ask them for examples.

Talk

Take a large sheet of paper and write on the top 'HOW TO GET YOUR OWN WAY'.

Ask the children how people get their own way and make other people do as they want.

Examples:
　Nagging.
　Saying they will not be your friend.
　Tricking you.
　Spoiling the game.

Write down some of their suggestions.

Comment

These are all methods people use to get their own way, but this is not a loving way to handle a friendship.

　Everyone has special things they want to do, but when people are friends it is not right that one person always gets his own way. In a friendship people take turns: sometimes you do what you want to do, sometimes you do what your friend wants to do. In the Bible it says that love does not insist on its own way.

Prayer

Help us to do what others want and not always insist on our own way.

A 12. Love Puts up with a Lot

You will need:

A pen, scissors, some red wool, a large sheet of card or sugar paper, Blu-Tak.

Introductory activity

Take down the next heart and complete the sentence so that it reads: 'Love … puts up with a lot'. Blu-Tak it inside the large heart.

Draw a large thermometer on a piece of paper. Mark a red bulb at the bottom, but do not mark in the red line.

Pierce a hole through the bulb and thread some red wool through it. Fix a piece of Blu-Tak to the end of the wool and fasten it to the bottom of the thermometer.

Talk

A thermometer is for testing a person's temperature – it tells the doctor how hot your body is.

This is a temper thermometer – it tests how hot a person's temper is.

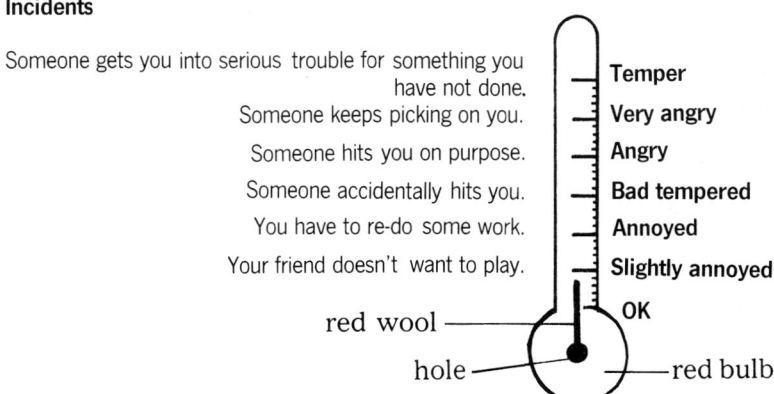

Ask the children about the type of things that slightly annoy them. Mark some on the thermometer.

Ask them about things that make them a bit cross. Mark them on the thermometer also.

Ask them about things which make them really angry. Mark some of them on the thermometer.

(Continued overleaf)

Take the red wool and pull it up the thermometer, reading the things that make a person more and more angry. Blu-Tak it at the top. Mark the top with the words BOILING POINT. Explain that if all these things happen to a person they might eventually lose their temper.

Comment

Some people have a very low boiling point, they lose their temper very early on. (Bring the red line down.) They get cross at every silly little thing. Love moves the boiling point right up; it puts up with a lot and does not explode over unimportant things.

Prayer

Help us, Lord, to keep our anger for the things that really matter – for injustice and unfairness, for defending others. Help us not to be irritable over every tiny thing.

A 13. Love Believes the Best

You will need:

A pen, Blu-Tak.

Love...
believes
the
best

Introductory activity

Take down the next heart and complete the sentence so that it reads: 'Love … believes the best'. Blu-Tak it inside the large heart.

Talk

This is a story about three chickens.

There were once three chickens who were very good friends and who always played together. Nearby lived a crafty fox who liked chicken for his dinner. However hard the fox tried he could never catch the three chickens; they stayed so close together that they always warned each other when the fox was coming. But the fox was very clever; he got his friend the grass snake to slip up to the chickens and whisper in each one's ear what the other chickens had been saying about her. The rumours the snake spread were quite untrue but the chickens began to believe the stories and soon they were all bad friends. They no longer played together, instead they played alone, and the fox enjoyed three lovely chicken dinners.

Comment

Love, says the Bible, believes the best about people, not the worst. It believes people are innocent until proved guilty.

Prayer

Help us to believe the best about people and not the worst. May we never spread tales about people that make others think badly of them.

A 14. Love Lasts

Love...
lasts

You will need:

A pen, Blu-Tak.
Packets of food with sell-by dates.

Introductory activity

Take down the next heart and complete the sentence so that it reads: 'Love … lasts'. Blu-Tak it inside the large heart.

Look at various packets of food and find out what their shelf life is.

Talk

Some items of food have a very short life (refer to an example), others have a very long life (refer to an example). The Bible says that love lasts; it does not need a date life on it because it will outlast anything else.

One famous writer put it like this, 'The good that men do lives after them'. In other words, no act of love is ever wasted: it goes on for ever.

The way we treat other people makes a difference to them, and in turn that will affect how they treat other people. Love lasts.

Comment

Sometimes adults get very concerned about not being famous or well known by others. The best way to be famous is to be known for the good that you do. Mother Teresa is a Yugoslavian nun. She is now very old. For many years she worked amongst the poor in India, completely unknown. Now Mother Teresa is very well known indeed, but even if she had not become famous she would never be forgotten by the people she has helped. Her work will never die.

Prayer

Help us to build a life based on love that will outlast anything else.

A 15. The Big Three

You will need:

A pen, paper, Blu-Tak.

Introductory activity

Take down the next heart and complete the sentence so that it reads: 'Love … is the greatest'. Blu-Tak it inside the large heart.

Have a vote on the three most popular: television programmes, foods, toys, games or sports, people (e.g. television personalities).

Do as many of these as you feel appropriate. In each case write up the most popular and the second and third choices.

Talk

The Bible says that the three greatest things in life are Faith (trust), Hope and Love, but the greatest of these is Love. The Bible describes each of these:

Faith
Faith is being sure of things we believe in, being certain of things we cannot see. It is like the dark side of the moon, we know it is there but we cannot see it.

Hope
Hope is a very strong word in the Bible. When we use the word about ordinary things we use it to mean 'maybe'. We might say, 'I hope it doesn't rain tomorrow.' We are not sure it will not rain. When the Bible talks of hope in God, however, it means certainty because God does not let people down. If Christians say, 'I hope God loves me' they mean 'I know God loves me'.

Love
Love is the central message of the Bible. Christians believe that God sent his son to live on the earth because he loved the world. If there is one word that sums up what God is like it is the word love. The Bible says, 'God is Love'.

Comment

The cross is used to remind Christians of faith, hope and love. The cross stands on three steps. Each step stands for one of these words. The top step is always love and for Christians the cross is a sign or symbol of love.

Prayer

There are many things in life that we need, Lord. Give us love more than anything else.

Follow-up Work for the Classroom

1. Make an alphabet of love or, for younger children, an acrostic poem using the word 'love'.

2. Do some 'Love isn't ...' work with the pupils. Ask them to suggest some things that love is not and illustrate these by examples.
   E.g. Love isn't selfish. Selfishness is when one person has a toy and she won't let anyone else play with it.

3. Make a 'Love is ...' book in which the children explore each aspect of love described in I Corinthians. Use a different page for each aspect and include stories, poems, invented situations, and pictures and cartoons.

B 1. Whom Do You Obey?

You will need:

Paper, Blu-Tak, pens.

Introductory activity

Write several 'commands' on the paper and write a list of people on the opposite side.

STOP TALKING	BABY BROTHER
SIT DOWN	TEACHER
BE QUIET	YOUNGER SISTER
GO TO SCHOOL	GRANNY
COME IN FOR TEA	MUM AND DAD
OBEY THE LAW	PRIME MINISTER

Ask the children which command they would obey when one of these people said it. Draw lines to connect the relevant phrases.

Talk

Obedience is good as long as you obey the right sort of person. What sort of person should you not obey? Talk with the children about obeying only those people who have their welfare at heart and those with a certain right or authority.

Comment

We obey people who have certain rights to ask us to do things, such as parents, teachers, dinner ladies, police officers. We also obey those we love because we want to do as they ask. People are not afraid to obey people they know and trust not to hurt them. Obedience has to come with trust, you should never obey someone you do not trust or if someone asks you to do something you know to be wrong, even if it is a person in authority. 'Trust' means knowing a person wants only what is for your good.

Christians believe they can trust God because they believe he wants only what is best for them.

Prayer

Give us the wisdom to trust those who really love us and wish us well and to obey them out of love and consideration.

B 2. Facing Difficult Situations

Introductory activity

Discuss some things you can do and some things you can't.

Example: I can jump over a rope 20 centimetres high, but I can't jump over a rope 2 metres high.

Ask the children for suggestions of things they can or cannot do.

Story

Here is a story about a time when the Israelites thought the situation was too difficult for them.

David the shepherd boy had seven older brothers, many of whom were in the army. One day David's father, Jesse, asked him to go to the army camp and take his brothers some extra food. David took the food and set off for the camp. He was looking forward to seeing his brothers again.

When he arrived at the camp it was strangely quiet; there was certainly no battle going on. David soon found out why. An enormous Philistine called Goliath stood on the hill opposite and shouted to the Israelite soldiers, 'Who is going to fight me? Why are you all such cowards? If you win we will serve you, if I win you shall be our slaves!'

No one offered to fight Goliath which only made him more angry and the Israelite soldiers slunk off to hide in their tents.

David could not believe that no one was prepared to fight Goliath. 'This is not right,' he said. 'He is not stronger than our God. I will fight him.' Everybody started laughing, David was too small to fight Goliath and he was not a trained soldier. David insisted on being taken to the king and he persuaded the king to let him fight the enormous Philistine. 'I might be young and small,' David said to the king, 'but as a shepherd I have had to fight bears and lions. God has always helped me in the past and he will help me now.'

King Saul was reluctant to let David fight Goliath, but he finally agreed and offered to lend David his armour. David tried on the armour, it was big and heavy and he had difficulty in moving. David decided to fight without armour and to use his shepherd's sling instead. He went to a nearby stream and chose five smooth pebbles, then he went to meet Goliath. Goliath laughed when he saw David coming towards him with a shepherd's stick and a sling. 'How can you fight me?' said Goliath, 'You are no more than a boy!' David looked up at the enormous Philistine and said, 'You fight against me with your great spear and sword, but I fight against you in the name of God who is my strength.' With that David loaded his sling and swirled it around his head. The stone struck Goliath with great force and he fell dead.

Comment

The Israelite army gave up because they thought Goliath was too big a problem and they were quite right! David realized how big the problem was, but he turned to God because he believed God was bigger still and could help him. Christians believe they can still turn to God in difficult situations, knowing he is bigger than the biggest problem.

Prayer

Thank you, Father, that you are bigger than the biggest problem and care for the small and the weak.

B 3. Hearing Is Not Enough

Introductory activity

Set up a 'hearing test':

Clap several simple rhythms and ask children to repeat them.

Stand pupils at different distances away and ask them to close their eyes. Whisper the names of colours and see which children can hear.

Whisper various instructions and ask children to do what they hear.

Story

This story was told by Jesus and is all about listening and doing as well.

The parable of the two houses
There were two men who built their houses on very different foundations. One man built his house on solid rock; it was hard work digging foundations into rock but he knew it would make the house secure. The second man could not be bothered to go to all that trouble so he built his house on sandy soil which was easier to dig.

   Both men finished their houses and moved in. One day it began to rain heavily, the river flooded and the house on sand collapsed. The house built on rock survived because it had solid foundations.

Comment

Jesus said that his words were like a strong rock that people could build their lives on, but hearing his words alone is not enough – they need to be obeyed. Christians believe the stories Jesus told were meant to change how people behaved; they were not just good stories.

   Listening is not much good without doing. If the lollipop lady tells you not to cross the road, it is no use hearing her unless you also do as she says.

Prayer

Help us to listen to the stories that Jesus told in a way that makes a difference to the way we behave.

B 4. Trusting God when You Don't Feel Brave

You will need:

A recording of the theme from 'Superman', if possible. Pictures of various superheroes, such as Super Ted and He-Man (ask the children to bring them in). Large sheets of paper.

Introductory activity

Show the pictures of various superheroes and spend some time talking with the children about the type of things they do. Tell them you are going to create a new superhero together. Invent a name and some special powers for the character.

Story

It's fun to dream of being a superhero or heroine: then we could solve all our difficulties instantly. But life is not like that for ordinary people. In real life many heroes and heroines are ordinary people who do extraordinary things. Here is a story about a hero in the Bible who definitely was not a superhero!

Gideon was chosen by God to rescue the Israelites from their enemies, who were called the Midianites. But Gideon was not a superhero, in fact he was no sort of hero at all. God chose Gideon for an important job and immediately Gideon thought there must be some mistake. 'You can't want me to rescue the country,' he said. 'I'm not brave or important enough.'

God assured Gideon that he would defeat the Midianites, but Gideon was not convinced. The last time the Midianites had raided his farm he had hidden from them. God assured Gideon that he would not need to be brave or strong, he would only need to trust him. Still Gideon was not convinced and he only agreed after much persuading.

Gideon finally got an army together and was very surprised when God told him he had too many men. 'I want the Israelites to know that it is my power which will save them and not their own strength,' said God. 'Tell anyone who is afraid to go home.' Twenty-two thousand soldiers went home, leaving Gideon with only ten thousand. Surprisingly God said, 'You still have too many soldiers, take your men down to the river and I will tell you who can stay and fight and who should go home.' When they were down at the river God said, 'Separate those who lap the water with their tongues like a dog from those who cup the water in their hand to drink.' Gideon sent home all those who lapped like a dog, for you cannot see the enemy if your face is in the water. This left him with three hundred men.

'Don't worry,' said God. 'I will give you the victory.' Gideon and his three hundred men won their battle in a most unusual way. At night they crept up to the Midianites' camp. Each of the Israelites had a torch, a trumpet and a large jar, as well as their weapons. They surrounded the enemy camp, covering their torches with the jars. When Gideon gave the signal they smashed the jars, made as much noise as possible with the trumpets and waved their torches. The enemy thought they were surrounded by a vast army and in the confusion they began to fight each other.

Comment

Gideon was no superhero but God used him to save his people. We are not superheroes, most of us are not heroes or heroines of any sort, but Christians believe that you do not have to be a hero to do an important job. God picks all sorts of people to do important jobs and gives them the strength that they need.

Prayer

Thank you, God, that you give people the strength they need to face difficult situations. We thank you for the example of Gideon who, though he was very frightened, trusted you.

B 5. *Trusting God for the Unknown*

You will need:

A few pieces of camping equipment if you have them, such as a lilo and a sleeping bag.

Introductory activity

Talk about camping.
What is it like camping in the rain?
What would it be like to camp all the time?
What would you miss if you lived in a tent the whole time?

Story

Abraham was a friend of God, he had known him for a long time. Abraham and his family lived in a town called Ur where they had everything they could want. One day God asked Abraham to move, to take his whole family including his nephew, and go to an unknown land. It would be a tremendous change for them all, living in tents as wanderers, but Abraham trusted that God knew what he was doing. Abraham packed his bags, organized his family and they all moved into the unknown land of Canaan. 'You might be a wanderer now,' said God, 'but one day I will give you a land of your own. Trust me.' That is exactly what Abraham did and finally one day he did have a land of his own, but for many years he and his family wandered about, living in tents and never settling for too long in one place.

Comment

God asked Abraham to do a very difficult thing, but Abraham knew God well enough to trust him even though it meant a great change in his way of life. Christians believe that they can trust God for the unknown future. They do not know what will happen in the future, but God does and he loves and cares for people.

Prayer

May we trust you as Abraham did, knowing that you have our good at heart.

(**Note:** Muslims know Abraham as the prophet Ibrahim, and Muslim children are likely to be familiar with the story.)

B 6. Reluctant Obedience

Introductory activity

Ask the children to think of all the different things people say when they want to get out of a job. Write some of them down.

Examples:
  No.
  Later.
  I'm busy.
  Do I have to?
  Karen's mum doesn't make her wash up.

Story

When God asked Jonah to tell the people of Nineveh to stop fighting, Jonah said, 'NO!' You could hardly blame him because the people of Nineveh had a terrible reputation. God looked at the way they hurt each other and everybody else and decided he would have to do something about it. He asked Jonah to go to Nineveh and tell the people that unless they changed their behaviour the city would be destroyed. 'Maybe that will stop them,' thought God.

Jonah had other plans; he could just imagine what the people of Nineveh would do if he arrived and told them to change or the city would be destroyed. Jonah was sure he would not survive. He thanked God politely and said, 'No.' He thought maybe God could find someone else to do the job, someone large and brave. God kept on asking Jonah, but still Jonah refused to go. Jonah decided he would have to get away, so he found a boat that was going as far away from Nineveh as possible and he got on board. 'Now I am safe,' thought Jonah. God, however, had not finished with Jonah. He caused a great storm and the sailors became afraid. 'God must be angry with someone,' they said. 'I'm afraid it's me,' said Jonah. 'You had better throw me overboard.' The sailors did not want to throw Jonah overboard but the storm became so bad they had no choice.

As Jonah sank he was swallowed by a large fish. Inside the belly of the fish Jonah had plenty of time to think; he decided to trust God and do as he asked. The fish eventually spat Jonah out on dry land and after a while Jonah made his way to Nineveh. The people of that town were just as bad as he expected but they did not attack him, instead they listened to what he had to say. The people were sorry for the way they had behaved and decided to change. God was delighted, the people were changed and the city was saved. It might all have happened sooner if Jonah had obeyed the first time.

Comment

Jonah tried hard to get out of the job God wanted him to do. He disobeyed God not because he did not trust God but because he was afraid. There is nothing wrong with fear, he was right to be afraid of the people of Nineveh, but he failed to ask God to help him with his fear. Christians believe that when God asks someone to do a job, he also gives them the strength they need to do it.

Prayer

When we are afraid, give us the courage we need to face unknown and difficult situations.

B 7. Obeying a Simple Command

Introductory activity

Play a short game of 'Simon Says' with a small group of children at the front.

Story

In the Bible there is a story about Naaman, who obeyed what sounded like a rather silly command.

The story of Naaman

Naaman was a commander of the Syrian army. He had a skin disease called leprosy and he and his wife were very upset about it because in those days there was no cure for leprosy.

Naaman's wife had a little Israelite slave girl who told them about the prophet Elisha who healed people by the power of God. Naaman took lots of treasure with him and went to find Elisha. Naaman's chariot stopped outside Elisha's house but the prophet did not come out, instead he sent a message to Naaman which said. 'Go and wash seven times in the River Jordan and your skin will be clear.' Naaman was furious. 'Why didn't he come to see me himself and anyway aren't there better rivers than the Jordan to bathe in back home?' Naaman stormed off in a temper. But his servants persuaded him to do as Elisha had said even though he did feel silly. He bathed seven times in the Jordan and came out cured. 'Now I believe in your God, please accept a gift as a token of thanks,' he said to Elisha. 'No,' said Elisha, 'It was God who healed you, not me.'

Comment

Naaman obeyed Elisha because he was persuaded to trust him. His little servant girl had told him that Elisha was a friend of God and God was powerful and loving. Christians believe they can trust God because he cares and he is wise so they are not afraid to obey him.

Prayer

Help us, Father, not to be so proud that we cannot ask for help or accept it when it is offered.

B 8. Doing What Is Right

Introductory activity

Talk about how some people try to get others in trouble. Ask the children how they do this.

Story

Daniel worked for the king, he was very good at his job and the king liked him. Daniel was also a friend of God and every day he talked to God and people could see him at his window praying. Some people were jealous of Daniel, they wanted to get him into trouble with the king so that he would lose his job. Each day they watched Daniel so that they could tell on him. For a long time they watched him but he never did anything to annoy the king. His enemies then thought up another plan. They decided to get the king to make a new law forbidding anyone to ask for help from anyone except the king himself. Anyone breaking this law would be thrown into the lions' den. Now they really could trap Daniel for they knew he would continue to ask God for help.

Daniel knew about the new law, but he continued to pray to God asking him for help to live his life. Straight away his enemies reported Daniel to the king. Daniel was taken to the palace where he freely admitted that he prayed to God and asked God to help him. The king realized it was a trap, but there was nothing he could do, for the laws of his country could not be altered. With much regret the king had Daniel put in the lions' den. All night the king worried while Daniel was with the lions, but Daniel was safe, God had closed the lions' mouths and Daniel came out the next morning unharmed. His enemies were dismayed, because Daniel became more popular with the king than ever.

Comment

Daniel's enemies succeeded in getting him into trouble, but Daniel trusted God and carried on praying. When we get into trouble we do not get thrown to the lions, but it can still be difficult to carry on doing what is right.

Prayer

Thank you, Father, for the example of Daniel who had the courage to carry on praying and trusted you for the outcome.

B 9. God with Us

Introductory activity

Talk with the children about situations when it helps to have someone with you.

Story

Shadrach, Meshach and Abednego were slaves in Babylon, a country which was ruled by the proud King Nebucadnezzer. One day Nebucadnezzer decided that everyone should bow down and worship his golden statue as a God. Shadrach, Meshach and Abednego knew that they could not do this for they were Israelites and worshipped the one God. They knew it was wrong to worship a man as a God even if he was the king! King Nebucadnezzer got all the people together and told them that when the trumpets played they must all bow down or be thrown into the fiery furnace.

The trumpets played and everyone bowed down except Shadrach, Meshach and Abednego. The king was furious, 'I'll give you one more chance,' he said, and once again the trumpets played and once again Shadrach, Meshach and Abednego refused to bow down. The three friends explained that they worshipped God and could not bow to a statue of gold. Nebucadnezzer asked them if they were afraid. They replied that they were but that God could save them and even if he didn't they still were not going to bow to a statue! Nebucadnezzer had them thrown into the furnace. But when he looked inside he saw they were unharmed and instead of three people in there, there were four. God was with them in the fire. Nebucadnezzer ordered them to come out and they came out of the furnace without any burns. The king could not believe what he saw: he threw three men into the fire and yet while they were in there he saw four men. God had let them go through the fire, but he had gone through it with them.

Comment

Nebucadnezzer was so impressed that he declared that the God of Shadrach, Meshach and Abednego was the true God and people should worship him.

Christians believe that God does not always protect people from every bad event or every danger, but they believe he never leaves their side.

Prayer

Thank you, Father, that you are with us in every situation in life – in the good times and the bad ones. May we trust that you are always by our side.

B 10. Keep Trusting

Introductory activity

Talk with the children about dangerous situations and obeying adults where safety is concerned.

Story

Peter had gone out fishing with his friends in a boat. While they were out a wind blew up and the waves became high. Suddenly the disciples saw Jesus walking towards them across the water. They were frightened because they thought he must be a ghost. Jesus reassured them he was not a ghost and Peter asked if he could walk to Jesus on the water. Peter kept his eyes on Jesus and stepped out of the boat and on to the water. Normally he would have sunk, but like Jesus he found he could walk on the waves. Then Peter stopped looking at Jesus and looked at the rough seas which surrounded him. The waves looked so big and frightening that Peter began to be afraid. He started to sink, but Jesus caught him and put him back in the boat.

Comment

Because he was God's special messenger Jesus could do things that we cannot do and that would be dangerous for us to try. Jesus had special powers to heal people and do miraculous things. Peter found he too could do more than he thought if he trusted Jesus. Peter sank when he stopped looking at Jesus and started looking at the size of the waves. Christians believe it is like that in life: if people only look at the problems they face it is easy to sink under fear as Peter sank under the sea. If people trust in God, who Christians believe is greater than any problem, they can do much more than they thought they could.

Prayer

Help us to trust you as Peter trusted Jesus. Help us to look at you more and to look less at the size of the problems we face.

Follow-up Work for the Classroom

1. Write out some of these stories and mount them on appropriate shapes, such as flames, waves, a tent.
2. Make an art display about 'Trust' by creating pictures for each story. Use a different technique for each one: printing, marbling, sponge painting, etc. Mount the display on the wall.

C 1. Not up to Standard

You will need:

A pair of balance scales. Some packets of things to weigh (with the weights printed on them). Make sure that some are deliberately short in weight.

Introductory activity

Practise weighing some things with the children (use the packets you have *not* tampered with). Explain how weights are written on the packets of items we buy. Show some examples and ask children to read out how much they weigh. Then weigh them to check that they are the correct weight. Explain that if something is underweight the manufacturer can get into trouble with the law. Weigh some things that are short on weight.

Story

King Belshazzar was a very proud man and thought he was more important than anyone else. One night he held a feast. The party went on for a long time and Belshazzar got very drunk. He sent for the golden bowls which his father had stolen from the Temple in Jerusalem. These bowls were used in the worship of God.

'I'm going to drink my wine from God's golden bowls because our gods and goddesses are more important than this God of the Jews,' he said. Belshazzar laughed but everyone else looked shocked. As he drank, a hand began to write on the wall. Belshazzar could not read the writing and he became extremely frightened.

'What does it say? What does it mean?' he asked.

No one had ever heard of anything like this happening before, but Belshazzar's mother remembered that Daniel lived nearby and he worshipped the God of the Jews. Belshazzar sent for Daniel to read the writing. 'I will give you gifts and riches, anything you want, if you will only tell me what the writing says,' pleaded Belshazzar.

'I don't want your riches, your majesty,' said Daniel, 'I will tell you what it says. It says NUMBER, WEIGHT and DIVISION. It means God has NUMBERED your days as king. You will not be king much longer because you have been WEIGHED in God's scales of goodness and justice and you have been found to be too light. There is not enough goodness in you. Your kingdom will be taken from you and DIVIDED between other people.'

Comment

Belshazzar was weighed by God and found to be too light. Like a bag of sugar that has had some taken out, he was only half full. This does not mean he was literally weighed, it means he was only half full of such things as love and goodness. It is picture language to say he was not up to God's standard. Christians believe that God weighs all people in his balances and he wants everyone to be up to his standard, he wants them to be full of goodness and love, not just half full. Christians believe that no one is completely up to God's standard, no one has quite enough love and goodness, but they do not worry that God will treat them as he treated Belshazzar. Christians ask God to help them come up to his standard; they ask him to fill them up with love.

Prayer

Help us, Father, to be full of love for others and not just half full.

C 2. *The Baby with a Job To Do*

You will need:
Some baby photographs, preferably of staff and pupils.

Introductory activity

Show the baby photographs and ask the children if they can recognize the babies. Ask the children to match the photos to the people.

Story

Here is a story about a baby who had a very important job to do. As a baby he looked the same as any other baby, but his life changed the history of a whole nation.

Many Israelites lived in Egypt because there was little food in their own land and they had moved south to Egypt to find food many years before. The king of Egypt feared such a large group of people living in his land so he made them slaves. The people worked very hard for no money and were very badly treated. The Israelites longed to be free but could find no way of escaping.

Although the king had made the Israelites slaves he was still afraid because there were so many of them. So he ordered the baby boys to be killed to reduce the number of Israelites. One family had just had a little boy and they kept him hidden from the soldiers, but he was growing fast and it was becoming more and more difficult to hide him.

The mother decided on a plan. She made a waterproof basket and put the baby in it. Miriam, the baby's sister, took the basket to the river and floated it in the water, amongst the rushes where the soldiers would not see it.

One of the princesses of Egypt came to the river to bathe and she saw the basket. She told her servants to fish it out of the water and open it up. Inside was the little Israelite baby. The princess wanted to keep the baby but she had no one to look after him. Miriam, who had been watching, ran out of the bushes and told her that she knew someone who would help her look after the baby. Miriam ran to fetch her mother who went to the palace and offered to care for the child, her own son, and so the baby was kept safe.

The baby was called Moses and he grew up in the royal palace. Although he grew up as an Egyptian prince he never forgot that he was really an Israelite. When he was much older God told him that he had a special job for him to do: he was to help set his people free from slavery. The baby who was so very nearly captured by the soldiers lived to do a very important job.

Comment

You cannot tell by looking at photographs what babies will be like when they grow up, because they all look much the same. To God each one is special, each has a different job to do. Christians believe that God has a job for each person; it may not be a spectacular job like that of Moses, but it will be a necessary one.

Prayer

Thank you, Father, that you knew each one of us as a baby and have given each of us the abilities to do the job you have for us.

C 3. Invisible Gifts

You will need:

Boxes of various sizes for the children to unwrap, inside each should be toys. Three boxes should be empty except for a piece of card on each of which is written one of the words – WISDOM, LOVE, JOY.

Introductory activity

Tell the children to pretend it is your birthday and you would like them to help you open your presents. Ask them to read the labels carefully first so that the other children can hear. Look very puzzled when three of the boxes are opened and found to be empty except for the pieces of card. Ask the children to turn them upside down and shake them to make sure there is no present inside.

Hold up each of the real presents and elaborate on how much you like them. Hold up the three cards and explain that they are invisible presents but they are more valuable than the others. Teddies and transformers might be fun but you can live without them. You can't live without LOVE, WISDOM (the ability to tell right from wrong) and JOY.

Story

Solomon's gift

Solomon became king when he was still a young man. He felt very young and small. Being king was a big job to take on and he desperately wanted to be a good king.

God wanted to give Solomon a present but he thought that Solomon should choose it himself. One night Solomon lay asleep and he dreamt that God had told him he could have any gift he asked for. Solomon thought about all the things he wanted. He could ask for gold and be the richest king in history. He could ask for weapons and rule many kingdoms. He could ask for great armies and be extremely powerful, he could ask for many slaves and never have to work hard. Solomon thought carefully about his reply to God. 'David my father was a great king, by comparison I feel like a little child. I am king over many people and to be a good king I need to know how to rule honestly and wisely so that the people will be happy and content. I need the gift of wisdom.' God was pleased when Solomon chose the gift of wisdom for it would mean he would be able to tell right from wrong and know how to choose the right.

Comment

Solomon chose his gift of wisdom because he wanted to rule his people well and he soon found his dream had come true. God gave Solomon great wisdom, but because he had asked for a gift that would help others, God also rewarded him many other gifts which he had not asked for. Solomon's wisdom became famous; not only was he wise himself, he collected wise sayings from many people to increase his wisdom. Some of Solomon's wise sayings are recorded in the Bible in the book of Proverbs.

Prayer

Give us the invisible gift of wisdom so that we too may know how to choose the right and reject what is wrong.

C 4. Super Vision

You will need:
Several items inside boxes, bags or wrapped in material. Example: a key wrapped in a scarf.

Introductory activity

Ask how many children have seen the 'Superman' films.

Tell the children that you are going to test to see if any of them are really supermen/women disguised as children.

Ask them what is unusual about Superman's eyes (he can see through almost anything). Ask them what he can't see through (lead).

Ask several children to look at the wrapped items and say whether they can see what is inside. Can they see through metal, paper or cloth?

Story

There is a story in the Bible about super vision.

God told the prophet Samuel that the country needed a new king. He told Samuel to go to the family of Jesse and he would find the new king there amongst Jesse's sons. So Samuel set off for Bethlehem where Jesse lived. When Samuel arrived at the farm he asked Jesse if he could see all his sons. Samuel looked at them – there were seven tall, strong, handsome lads. He looked at each one; any of them might have made a future king, but as he stopped by each boy God said, 'No, not this one.' Samuel reached the end of the line and God had said 'No' to all of them.

'Have you got any more sons, Jesse?' he asked. 'Only little David, my youngest,' said Jesse. 'He's out in the fields with the sheep.' Samuel asked Jesse to call him in.

Samuel looked at David – he was a good-looking boy but he was young and inexperienced, he was only a shepherd. The other brothers were experienced soldiers, tough and strong. 'This is the one,' said God. Samuel was surprised. He took out the special oil and poured a little on David's head; that was how all kings of Israel were made king. David knew now that one day in the future he would be the king, but he could be patient, he knew he would have to wait.

Samuel wondered why God had not chosen any of the other brothers to be king. God told him that his eyes were not like ours, he did not look at the outside of a person to see how well they were dressed, what they looked like or whether they were short or tall, thin or fat. God's eyes looked at the inside of a person to see their heart, whether they were good and loving, honest and brave.

Comment

Superman might have X-ray vision and see things we cannot see but Christians believe that God can see further than that, into the human heart.

Prayer

Thank you, Father, that you look at a person's inside and not their outside.

C 5. Hope

You will need:
Some paper 'bones', sellotape and if possible a recording of the song 'Them bones, them bones'.

Introductory activity

Play 'Them bones' as the children come in. Ask them to listen carefully to the words.

Make two sets of leg bones and one hip bone by drawing large copies of the bones illustrated. Cut out the bones.

Ask several children to come out to the front. Explain that they are going to put the bones together, using sellotape.

Talk about bones and the job they do. They are vital but by themselves they do not live, they only live as part of a living body.

Story

Here is a story about a strange type of dream dreamt by a man called Ezekiel.

The people of Israel were unhappy, their love of life and all their hopes were dead. Their country had been invaded and many people had been killed, while others had been made into slaves. The people were thoroughly miserable; fun, laughter, hope and happiness had all died out in Israel.

When everything looked hopeless God sent Ezekiel a special dream. Ezekiel saw in his dream a lot of dry old bones, lifeless and lying about on the ground. As Ezekiel watched, the bones came to life. The bones connected to each other and became a skeleton. The skeleton grew muscles and skin and became a living human being. Ezekiel had never had such a strange dream and he wondered what it meant.

God told him the meaning of this special dream. 'The people of Israel are lifeless and without hope just like those dry bones, but just as I made the dry bones live in the dream so I will make the people of Israel live again and be happy and hopeful. I rescued them once before when they were unhappy and in slavery and I will do it again.'

Comment

When everything looked bad for the Israelites God gave them hope and they trusted him for their future. In time they were rescued from slavery and went back home again: Ezekiel's dream came true. Christians believe they can still trust God to look after them in the future even though they do not know what is going to happen, for they believe that God does know what will happen in the future and they trust a loving and wise God.

Prayer

Thank you, Father, that we can still trust you for the future even when the situation looks hopeless.

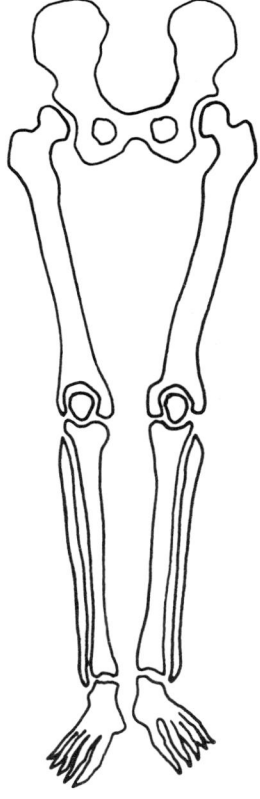

Follow-up Work for the Classroom

1. Make a zig-zag book using some of these stories.

2. Make a gift box display, printing your own wrapping paper for the boxes. It can be two- or three-dimensional. Ask the children to think of different invisible gifts and on each box write the name of the invisible gift it contains.

NOTE: Some of the assemblies in this group contain quite difficult ideas and may not be suitable for infants.

D 1. What Is a Prophet?

You will need:
Some newspapers and a calendar.

Introductory activity

Talk about how we find out what has happened during the day. Ask the children for suggestions (radio, television, newspapers, etc.).

All of these things tell us what happened during the day or what happened yesterday or last week. They do not tell us what will happen tomorrow.

Story

Many people would like to know what will happen tomorrow or in the future and some try to guess.

A prophet's job was to tell the people what God told him about the future. A prophet passed the message on.

Here is one thing that a prophet called Jeremiah said about the future of the Jewish people when they were very sad because they had suffered so much. Many people had died in battle and others were taken as prisoners to a far-off land.

'I have great plans for you, plans that will be for your good. I will give you a future and a hope ... You will be a great nation again and I will bring back those who have been captured and taken away as slaves.'

Comment

Telling the people about the future was only a small part of a prophet's job; tomorrow we will look at the other half of his work.

Prayer

Thank you, Lord, for the prophets who faithfully told others about you, sometimes telling of events they did not live to see.

D 2. Pass the Message on

You will need:
A piece of paper, an envelope and a pen.

Introductory activity

Write a simple message on the paper and place it in the envelope. Address the envelope to someone in the assembly.

Give the written message to a child and ask them to pass it to their neighbour and tell them to pass it on to their neighbour until it reaches the person whose name is on the envelope. It does not really matter what the message says.

Play 'pass the message on' using a verbal message passed down a line of children. They must listen carefully and repeat the message accurately.

Talk

The main part of a prophet's job was to tell the people about God and how he wanted them to live. Some of the prophet's messages were very practical: they told the people to stop cheating and lying, they told them God loved them or that God was angry when he saw people hurting each other.

Here are some of the messages the prophets passed on:

What does God want you to do? He wants you to be fair, to forgive others and to be his friend. (Micah)

I hate your singing and I can't stand your services. How can I enjoy your worship when you treat the poor so badly? (Amos)

Comment

The prophets had a hard job, often they had difficult messages to pass on or messages that made them unpopular. Although their messages were spoken to people thousands of years ago, what they said is still valued by Christians today.

Prayer

Thank you for the prophets who passed the message on. Thank you for their courage when they had to deliver messages that were not popular. May we also have the courage to do what is right, even if it is not what everyone else is doing.

D 3. The Plumb Line (Amos)

You will need:
A plumb line or spirit level, string and plasticine.

Introductory activity

Demonstrate the use of a plumb line and a spirit level. Talk about how and why they are used.

Make a plumb line with a length of string and a ball of plasticine.

Story

One day Amos had a strange dream. He imagined God with a plumb line, standing beside a wall and examining it to check it was straight. The plumb line showed that the wall was straight, it had been built properly.

Comment

We sometimes use the word 'crooked' to mean something that is wrong. A 'crook' is also another word for a criminal. God gave Amos this message:

'My people are like a wall that has been built wrongly. It is crooked.'

Amos passed the message on, he told the people that God was sad and angry because they had built their lives on lies, greed and cruelty. They were like a crooked wall, they needed to be rebuilt.

Christians believe that Amos's message is still relevant today: people should build their lives on love, honesty and friendship with God, then they will make God happy.

Prayer

May we be built straight and true like a wall that is built with a plumb line. May we build our lives on love, justice and friendship with you.

D 4. Baby Reins (Hosea)

You will need:

A pair of baby reins.

If possible, a baby who has just begun to walk, or a toddler, and a parent.

Introductory activity

Talk about teaching a child to walk or interview a parent about this.

Show the reins and try them on the baby, if one is present.

Talk

Helping a baby to walk is a difficult process. Babies need to learn to walk, but their parents do not want them to hurt themselves or walk anywhere dangerous. Sometimes parents use baby reins to help a child who is learning to walk; sometimes they support the child with their arms.

This is how the prophet Hosea described God:

I love my people like a parent loves a young child. As a parent shows their love when they feed a baby and teach it to walk so I love my people. I take them in my arms and my baby reins are love and kindness.

Comment

Hosea does not mean God literally took people in his arms, he means that God is there, loving, protecting and helping his people just as a parent does. Christians believe that God is still there loving and protecting people even if he cannot be seen.

Prayer

Thank you, Father, for your love and care. You love us more than even the best earthly father could. May we love you in return.

D 5. The Heart Transplant (Ezekiel)

You will need:
A drawing of a heart.

Introductory activity

Talk about where the heart is in the body and what it does.

Talk about what it is made of. The heart is a muscle. Pupils can feel the muscles in their arms or legs to get an idea of its texture.

Talk about heart transplants briefly.

Talk

People used to think that a person's feelings were in the heart. If someone was cruel and nasty they were sometimes called 'hard-hearted'. If someone was kind and gentle they were sometimes called 'soft-hearted'.

Many people in Israel at the time of the prophet Ezekiel were cruel and hard-hearted so God sent this message to Ezekiel to pass on to the people:

I will give you a new heart ... I will take out your stony (hard) heart and give you a soft heart of flesh.

Comment

This did not mean that God was going to do an operation like a heart transplant. God was saying that he was going to change them from being hard-hearted (cruel/stony) to being soft-hearted (loving/flesh). Christians believe that God does a special 'heart transplant'. He changes how people feel on the inside, which in turn changes how they behave. God's heart transplant is invisible: it is a change in feelings and actions.

Prayer

Forgive us, Father, when we are hard-hearted and refuse to help others. Give us a soft heart that will love you and respond to those in need.

D 6. Can a Leopard Change its Spots? (Jeremiah)

You will need:
Pictures of a leopard, a lion and a tiger.

Introductory activity

Talk about leopards and the difference between lions, tigers and leopards (spots, stripes and unmarked).

A leopard is permanently marked as a leopard by its skin, it cannot change and become a tiger or a lion.

Talk

Jeremiah was given a very strange message by God. Here is what he had to tell the people:

Can a leopard change its spots? Neither can you change your behaviour. You are so used to doing wrong that you find it impossible to change the way you live.

Comment

Jeremiah did not like giving this message to the people, as it was a warning. He told them that God would not ignore their behaviour for ever. However, Jeremiah also had a cheerful message: he told the people that God would help them change – unlike the leopard they were not stuck permanently in one state.

Prayer

Thank you, Father, that with your help we can change. Help us to be more like you.

D 7. Drops in a Bucket (Isaiah)

You will need:
A bucket of water and a spoon.

Introductory activity

Ask the children to watch very carefully as you drop one single drop of water from a spoon. Repeat this several times.

Talk about how small a drop is. Ask the children to guess how many drops make a whole bucketful of water. (You can calculate this by measuring how many drops make 20 ml and then doing the appropriate sum!)

Talk

The people of Israel were very frightened. All the nations around them were bigger and fiercer than they were. The other nations had big armies with modern weapons and they were not afraid to use them. Each night the news was terrible.

God gave the prophet Isaiah this message:

Don't worry about the bad news. Don't worry about all these fierce nations, they are no more than a drop in a bucket to God.

Comment

A drop is very small compared to the total amount in the bucket. The nations around them looked very big and frightening to the Israelites, but to God they looked very small indeed. God assured Israel that he had the situation under control. Christians today believe that God is ultimately in control, each nation is still no more than a 'drop in a bucket'.

Prayer

When the news frightens us help us to remember that you are bigger than all the nations and that in the end good will triumph.

D 8. The Long Arm (Isaiah)

You will need:
Several adult volunteers and some children. Paper and pens (optional).

Introductory activity

Compare the length of different people's arms.

Compare the span of different people's hands. Draw around them if you wish.

Talk

Sometimes having a long arm is useful. If someone needed rescuing you could reach out your arm and stretch out your hand to help them. When Israel was in trouble and needed rescuing from its enemies, Isaiah was given this message:

Don't worry, God has not got a short arm, he can rescue you.

Comment

The Israelites were in trouble and needed help, and Isaiah told them that God could save them. Using words, he drew a picture of God. God is like a person standing on a river bank, when someone has just fallen in the water: God reaches out his arm and stretches open his hand to rescue them. Christians believe God is still like that today, always ready to help and save.

Prayer

Thank you, Father, that you have a long arm and an outstretched hand that is always ready to help us.

D 9. The River of Justice (Amos)

You will need:
Paper and pens; a large map of the world, if possible.

Introductory activity

Ask the children the names of any rivers they know.

Point out some of the large rivers of the world on the map.

Talk

There are many rivers and streams that we know, real rivers that flow through real countries. The prophet Amos spoke of an imaginary river. He said this:

Let justice flow like a river and righteousness like a never-ending stream.

Comment

Amos's river had two names – it was the river of justice and the river of righteousness. It was an invisible river. Justice means fairness; righteousness means the type of behaviour that creates right friendships – right friendships with God and with other people. Just as we need ordinary rivers to give the land life so Christians believe that every country needs Amos's invisible river of justice and righteousness.

Prayer

Forgive us, Father, when we ignore injustice and treat others badly. Give us the strength to work for what is right and good.

D 10. Ink Stain (Isaiah)

You will need:
A piece of cloth with a red ink stain.

Introductory activity

Talk about staining clothes.

Sometimes lids are left off felt-tip pens and the ink spreads over clothes and tablecloths. Sometimes we spill things and they leave a stain. Stains such as ink, blackberry and beetroot can be hard to get out. Stains spoil things, they can make good clothes look terrible. Your best dress will not look very good with a beetroot stain down the front, neither will your new anorak look all right with an ink stain on it.

Talk

God gave this message to Isaiah to pass on to the people:

Though the wrongs you have done stand out like a bright red stain on a piece of white cloth, I will wash it until it is as white as snow.

Comment

Just as a stain spoils a good garment, so wrong spoils a person's life. God told the people not to give up, he would help them change. He would forgive their wrong and help them live differently in the future. It would be like washing a stain off clothes. Christians believe God still does this: he forgives the wrong people have done and helps them to change.

Prayer

Thank you, Father, that you forgive us when we do wrong and help us to change. Help us to forgive others when they wrong us.

Follow-up Work for the Classroom

1. Stain some paper cream by dipping it in a solution of instant coffee. Screw up the paper and then smooth it out before you dip it. This 'ages the paper'. When the paper is dry the *teacher* can singe the edges to make them look damaged. Write some of the messages from the prophets on this paper and display them.

2. Cover a wall with frieze paper. Ask the children to write out some of the messages of the prophets and paint pictures of them. Pictures of buckets, leopards, walls, hands and hearts can be displayed.

E 1. Rules for Life

You will need:
A copy of the highway code.

Introductory activity

Ask the children for examples of school rules.

Talk about rules at home.

Read out to them some of the rules of the road.

Ask them what they think rules are for. Be specific. E.g. Why do parents say, 'No playing with matches'? Why does the school say, 'No running in the corridor'?

Talk

There are various types of rules. Some are safety rules. For example:

Do not play with matches.
Don't touch hot things.
Look before you cross the road.

These rules are there to protect us.

Some rules help us to live together in peace. For example:

No stealing.
No fighting.
No trespassing.

Here is what the Bible says about God's rules:

Your rules are like a torch that shows me the way on a dark road.
They help me decide between right and wrong.
The rules you have given are fair and just.
Your rules keep us safe so that we do not fall.

(Adapted from Psalm 119)

Comment

Rules can be unnecessary and can spoil life if there are too many of them or if they are about unimportant things. Rules are meant to make life better and safer for everyone.

Prayer

Thank you, Father, for those rules which make life better and improve the way we live.

E 2. Negative Rules

You will need:
A large sheet of paper, a pen.
Some items to choose between (such as books, sweets).

Introductory activity

Invite several children to make choices between the items you offer them.

Talk

Every time we make a choice we say no to one thing and yes to something else. If we have to make a choice and we say yes to one book, we say no to the other. If we say yes to one sweet, we say no to the other because we cannot always have everything, sometimes we have to choose.

In life we have to make choices about how we are going to behave.

If we say NO to lying, we say YES to truth and YES to being trusted.

If we say NO to cheating, we say YES to honesty.

If we say NO to hate, we say YES to love.

If people say NO to stealing, they say YES to respecting other people's property.

In the Bible there are some rules which start with a NO, or DON'T, such as:

Do not lie.
Do not steal.
Do not murder.

They are really YES rules.

Do speak the truth.
Do respect other people's property.
Do let everyone live in safety.

Comment

Many people are discouraged when they see 'NO' rules. It is sometimes helpful to ask yourself what these rules are really saying YES to. Christians believe that God made rules to make life better not worse.

Prayer

Thank you, Father, for those NO rules which say YES to so much that is good in life.

E 3. Positive Rules

You will need:
A large sheet of paper, pens.

Introductory activity

'YES' rules start with words like YOU MUST or DO.

Ask the children for examples of YES rules from home and school; they must not have the words 'can't', 'don't, or 'no' in them. Write a few on the paper or use an overhead projector.

Talk

What happens when we cross out the positive part of the rule and make it read the opposite to what was intended?

Try this with all the positive rules you have written. Write them up in one colour pen and then cross out 'Do' and replace it with 'Don't' in another colour pen.

DO (don't) HELP MUM WITH THE WASHING UP.
DO (don't) DRIVE SLOWLY IN TOWNS.
DO (don't) STOP AT TRAFFIC LIGHTS.

What would life be like if these YES rules became NO rules?

Comment

Good rules say YES to what is good and right in life. Christians believe that the YES rules are there to help people live in friendship with God and with each other.

Here are some of the YES rules from the Bible.

Do love God.
Do love your neighbour.
Do speak the truth.
Do love and respect your parents.

Prayer

Thank you, Father, for these rules which enable us to live together peacefully.

E 4. Breaking the Rules

Introductory activity

Talk about breaking the rules and what happens when we break rules – at home, at school and on the road.

Talk

For Christians breaking God's rules is not just breaking a regulation or law, they believe it hurts God's feelings. Christians believe that God made and loves all people, therefore anyone who steals from another person or hurts them in any way also hurts God. It is like your parents feeling angry and upset if you have your bike stolen or if you are hit by another pupil. They have not been hurt but they feel angry and upset because this action has hurt their child whom they love.

Anything that hurts his people also hurts God. Doing wrong is not just breaking the rules for a Christian, it is breaking a friendship.

Breaking the rules is not unforgivable; Christians believe that God is always ready to forgive people and help them change.

Here is a psalm about breaking the rules.

The Lord looks down at all that people do,
He looks to see who is wise and who worships him,
But he sees instead people doing every kind of wrong.
'Don't they know how to live?' says God.
'They live by robbing my people and they never pray to me.'

(Adapted from Psalm 53)

Comment

In this psalm God is upset to see the way people live, he is hurt to see his people robbed and badly treated. Christians believe that when someone breaks the rules and hurts another human being, God also feels hurt and it damages their friendship with him.

Prayer

Thank you, Father, that you care so much about us that you are hurt when someone hurts us.

E 5. Pictures of Rules

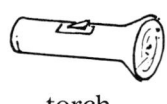
torch

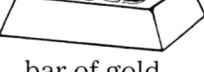
bar of gold

pot of honey

You will need:
Paper, pens.

ball and chain

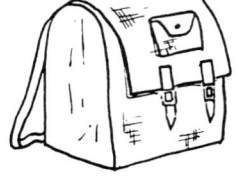
heavy burden

Introductory activity

Draw a larger version of these drawings.

Ask the children what each of the drawings is.

Tell them that each drawing is a way of describing rules. Can they guess what each drawing is saying about rules? Ask them for suggestions.

Talk

All these pictures are ways of looking at God's rules. Some people think that God's rules are a heavy burden, spoiling the fun. Others look upon them as a ball and chain, they feel imprisoned by rules, they feel they cannot do the things they want to do.

Christians, however, describe rules as a torch on a dark night. Just as a torch shows you the path on a dark night and stops you falling into danger, so God's rules show people how to live and stops them falling into such dangers as stealing and lying.

Christians also describe God's laws as honey, something sweet and good, and as gold, something extremely precious. They believe God's rules make life sweeter and better.

Comment

Some of these pictures are negative feelings about rules, some are positive. Ask the children to indicate which pictures express a **good** feeling and which ones express a **bad** feeling. Explain that for the Christian God's rules are something that frees them to live as he wants them to.

Prayer

Thank you, Father, for rules that free us to enjoy life without hurting others.

Follow-up Work for the Classroom

1. Ask the children to make up their own rules for living. Make a display of their rules.

2. Find out some more of God's rules (the Ten Commandments). Put these in a form the children will understand.

F 1. Getting a Job

You will need:
Some job adverts from the local newspaper.

Introductory activity

Read out some job descriptions from the local paper.

Talk

When Jesus first started his job he read a description of it in the Bible which had been written many years before. Here is what it said.

> God has given me a special job to do.
> He has sent me to tell the poor the good news,
> to bandage up the broken-hearted people,
> to comfort the sad,
> to give sight to the blind,
> and to set the captives free.

When John the Baptist wanted to know if Jesus was God's special king, Jesus sent him a message:

> Tell John:
> the blind receive their sight,
> the lame walk,
> those who have leprosy are cured,
> the deaf hear,
> the dead are brought to life,
> the good news is preached to the poor.

Jesus was telling John that he was God's special messenger and doing the job he had been sent to do.
If we put these two lists together we can see what Jesus's job was.

Write up this list:

> To give sight to the blind.
> To make the lame walk.
> To give hearing to the deaf (and speech to those who could not talk).
> To heal the sick.
> To bring the dead back to life.
> To comfort the sad.
> To preach the good news to the poor.
> To set the prisoners free.

(Continued overleaf)

Comment

This was a very strange job description! If we look at what Jesus did during his life we can see how he carried out this difficult job. Christians believe he fulfilled his job, he told people about the good news of God's love and forgiveness, he gave the blind their sight, he made the lame walk and the deaf hear. Deafness is often associated with being unable to speak because if people cannot hear they find it hard to learn language. Jesus not only cured the deaf, he gave speech back to those who could not talk. He cured leprosy sufferers, he gave life back to some who had died and he comforted the broken-hearted. He did not open prison doors and release criminals, but he set free people who were prisoners of wrong and evil.

During assemblies over the next two weeks we will tick off one of these subjects each day as we explore how Jesus did his job.

Prayer

Help us, Father, to carry on Jesus's job of spreading the good news and helping those who are hurt whether from illness or from other things that have happened to them.

F 2. Spreading the Good News

You will need:
Newspapers.

Introductory activity

Tick off the appropriate part of the job description.

Show the children the headlines in some local newspapers. (Choose them with care!)

Ask them what sort of things would make *good* news.

Talk

Jesus went around Palestine spreading the good news about God. He told people how much God loved them, how God wanted them to live and how to join God's family.

Jesus described spreading the message about God like a man sowing seed. The farmer sows his seed and whether he sleeps or whether he watches over it once it is sown all he can do is wait to see if it grows. The farmer cannot force the seed to grow. The seed falls into the soil and grows, producing plants which in turn produce many more seeds. The farmer plants the seed, but it is God who makes it grow.

Jesus said that he and his followers are like farmers spreading the good news, as a farmer spreads seed on the soil. The words take root and grow in people's hearts and so the good news spreads and God's family or kingdom grows.

Sing the song 'Oats, peas, beans and barley grow'.

Oats, peas, beans and barley grow.
Oats, peas, beans and barley grow.
Nor you, nor I, nor anyone know,
How oats, peas, beans and barley grow.

First the farmer sows the seed,
Then he stands and takes his ease,
Stamps his feet and claps his hands,
And turns around to view his land.

(Repeat the first verse.)

Comment

Jesus spread the good news by talking to people. Today Christians spread the good news by television and radio, by books and magazines and posters, as well as by talking to one another.

Prayer

Thank you, Father, for the good news that Jesus brought – good news of love and forgiveness.

F 3. Comforting the Sad

You will need: Paper and pen.

Introductory activity

Tick off the appropriate part of the job description.
Talk about the things that sadden people.

Talk

Sometimes things happen which sadden us. Sadness, however, does not only come when we face difficult times, often we are sad because we worry about the future. We worry about things that might never happen. We may have nothing to make us sad now but we worry about things which might make us sad in the future.

A poet called Shel Silverstein wrote a poem called 'What if ...' and he drew some lovely cartoons of imaginary 'What if ...' monsters that creep into people's ears at night and make them worry. The monsters whisper things such as 'What if you can't do your maths?' 'What if you miss the bus to school?' The 'What if ...' monsters are not real, they are really our thoughts and worries disturbing us.

Whatif

Last night, while I lay thinking here,
Some Whatifs crawled inside my ear
And pranced and partied all night long
And sang their same old Whatif song:
Whatif I'm dumb in school?
Whatif they've closed the swimming pool?
Whatif I get beat up?
Whatif there's poison in my cup?
Whatif I start to cry?
Whatif I get sick and die?
Whatif I flunk that test?
Whatif green hair grows on my chest?
Whatif nobody likes me?
Whatif a bolt of lightning strikes me?
Whatif I don't grow taller?
Whatif my head starts getting smaller?
Whatif the fish won't bite?
Whatif the wind tears up my kite?
Whatif they start a war?
Whatif my parents get divorced?
Whatif the bus is late?
Whatif my teeth don't grow in straight?
Whatif I tear my pants?
Whatif I never learn to dance?
Everything seems swell, and then
The nighttime Whatifs strike again!

Shel Silverstein

Here is our 'What if ...' monster.

Draw a worried-looking monster. Ask the children to write around it some of the things it might be saying.

Jesus told people not to worry because God cared for them and knew all their needs. He said there are enough things to keep people busy each day without worrying about tomorrow.

Comment

Worry does not alter tomorrow, it only spoils today. It is all right to plan for tomorrow, but it is not good to worry about things that may not happen. Jesus comforted those who were sad through worrying by telling them that Christians believe God cares and is in control of all the tomorrows.

Prayer

Help us to live one day at a time and not spoil the time you have given us by worrying.

F 4. Giving Sight to the Blind

You will need:
A blindfold, some objects to feel.

Introductory activity

Tick off the appropriate part of the job description.

Talk a little about what it is like to be blind. Blindfold a child and ask him or her to handle the objects and guess what they are.

Ask the children to think very carefully about what it is like to be blind. What would they most miss seeing?

Talk

The blind man at Bethsaida

When Jesus was going through Bethsaida some people brought a blind man to him and asked Jesus to heal him. Jesus placed his hands on the blind man's eyes and asked the man if he saw anything. The man looked up. 'I see people,' he said. 'They look like trees walking.' Jesus covered the man's eyes once more and this time when the man looked up he could see clearly.

Comment

Jesus healed the man's eyes and for the first time the man could see the world around him. How strange it must be to see the world for the first time as an adult or to see the world after having lived in darkness for a long time. Those of us with sight cannot begin to imagine what this must be like.

Prayer

Help us, Father, never to take our sight for granted but always to value it as a precious gift from you.

F 5. Setting the Prisoners Free

You will need:
Some toy handcuffs, large sheets of paper, pens, Blu-tak.

Introductory activity

Tick off the appropriate part of the job description.

Use the toy handcuffs and talk about being in prison. What would a prisoner most miss in prison?

Talk

Jesus did not open prison doors or unlock handcuffs. He did not set prisoners free in the sense of helping them escape from a building. Jesus set people free from invisible prisons: prisons of greed; prisons of selfishness; prisons of hate; prisons of envy.

People sometimes build their own prisons, they can be so selfish they are not free to give to others. Some can be so greedy they are not free to share. Others can be locked in a prison of hate so that they are not free to love. Some are trapped in a cell of envy so they are not free to enjoy what other people have without always wanting it for themselves.

What other prisons do people build for themselves?

Draw a prison cell with bars and ask the children to suggest the types of prison people build.

Comment

Jesus taught love and forgiveness, justice and truth. He taught about living as God wanted us to and caring for others. He set people free to love and serve each other.

Prayer

Help us to understand that love is the key that unlocks the prisons people make for themselves.

F 6. Making the Lame Walk

Introductory activity

Tick off the appropriate part of the job description.

Talk about disability. Explain that some people Jesus met were lame and unable to walk so they had to beg for a living. Discuss what activity a lame person would most want to do.

Talk

Jesus was walking by the pool of Bethesda. Disabled people often used to lie beside the pool, for they believed that it had healing powers and they might be cured if they could get into the water when it bubbled. Jesus saw a lame man lying there; he had been lame for thirty-eight years. Jesus asked the man if he wanted to be well and the man explained that he could not walk and he had no one to help him into the water. Jesus did not offer to help him into the water, instead he said, 'Stand up, pick up your mat and walk.' At once the man tried to get up and found he was cured.

Comment

We do not know the first thing the lame man did, but we do know that later that day he met Jesus in the Temple, so perhaps one of the first things he did was to say thank you to God.

Prayer

Help us, Father, never to take walking, running or dancing for granted.

F 7. Making the Silent Speak

Introductory activity

Tick off the appropriate part of the job description.

Declare two minutes silence and afterwards ask the children how difficult it is to keep silent.

Ask them to imagine what it must be like to be unable to speak. How would they communicate with other people? What things would they find most difficult?

Talk

Jesus met a man who was deaf and barely able to talk. His world was silent and he could not tell people what he wanted to say. Some friends brought the man to Jesus and begged him to heal the man. Jesus took the man away from the crowd; he touched his tongue and ears and looked up to heaven and said, 'Be opened!' Straight away the man could speak and hear.

Jesus told the man to keep quiet about what had happened but the man was so overjoyed that he spread the news far and wide.

Comment

We do not know what were the man's first words, but 'Thank you' might be a good guess. What do you think he would most want to say after he had thanked Jesus?

Prayer

Help us to be grateful for the gift of speech and to use this gift wisely. May our words heal and not hurt.

F 8. Making the Deaf Hear

You will need:

Some objects that make distinctive sounds: e.g. a crisp bag, a balloon being blown up, a cup of liquid being stirred with a spoon, a toy friction car being pushed along.

Introductory activity

Tick off the appropriate part of the job description.

Ask the children to be absolutely quiet. Tell them to close their eyes and listen for sounds outside the room. What can they hear?

Ask one child to come up to the front and close their eyes and try to guess what objects are from their sounds.

Ask the children what sound they think they would most miss if they could not hear. What sounds do they think they would not miss?

Talk

Refer to the previous story.

Comment

Often when Jesus cured people he told them to keep quiet about it. Why do you think he did this? Perhaps he thought that a reputation as a popular 'miracle worker' would not help his real work.

Prayer

Thank you, Father, for our hearing; for all the sounds we hear – the rustle of leaves and the din of traffic, the noise of the waves and the voices of our friends. May we never forget to thank you for our hearing.

F 9. Healing the Sick

You will need:
A bell.

Introductory activity

Tick off the appropriate part of the job description.

Explain that leprosy was once a widespread disease that could not be cured. Now it can be treated and is far less common. Because it was catching a person who had leprosy had to leave their family and go to live far away from others. They would ring a bell to warn others not to go near them (ring the bell). Ask the children to imagine the lonely lives these people led.

Talk

Jesus was walking in the countryside when a man who had leprosy approached him. The man knelt down and said to Jesus, 'If you want to, I know you can heal me.'

Jesus felt very sad to see the man so ill and so alone. 'Of course I want to,' replied Jesus and he touched the man. Immediately the man was cured.

Comment

Jesus not only cured the man, he also touched him; it had probably been a long time since anyone had had the courage to do that.

Prayer

Thank you, Father, for our health. May we never take it for granted.

F 10. *Bringing the Dead back to Life*

Introductory activity

Tick off the appropriate part of the job description.

NOTE TO THE TEACHER:
This assembly deals with death and should be handled sensitively. It might be as well to consult all staff first in case there are any recently bereaved children in the school.

Talk

When someone dies it is very sad, but in this story Jesus turned the parents' sadness into joy.

Jairus was an important man, he had many things but only one child. Jairus and his wife loved their little daughter and were very worried when one day she fell ill and rapidly got worse. Jairus had heard that Jesus healed the sick so he quickly ran to fetch him. He found Jesus and fell at his feet, 'Please come quickly,' he begged, 'My little girl is dangerously ill, she is dying.'

Jesus went with Jairus to his house but before he could reach it a messenger came and said to Jairus, 'Your daughter is dead, don't bother Jesus any more.' Jesus ignored the messenger and turned to Jairus, saying, 'Don't be afraid, just trust me.' Jesus went into the house where everyone was crying, and told the people to stop making such a noise. 'The child is not dead but asleep,' he said. When the people heard this they laughed at Jesus for they knew the little girl was dead.

Jesus went to the girl's bedside and took her by the hand, saying to her, 'Get up, little girl.' The girl got up and walked around. Her parents were overjoyed. Jesus told them to give her something to eat and to keep quiet about what had happened.

Comment

Jesus changed Jairus's grief to joy, he not only healed the daughter but her parents' broken hearts.

When Christians talk about Jesus raising the dead today they usually mean that death is not the end but the beginning of a new life with God which goes on for ever.

Prayer

Thank you, Father, for the story of Jesus healing Jairus's daughter. Help us to remember that death is not the end but only a beginning.

Follow-up Work for the Classroom

1. Make a display about the various parts of Jesus's job. This can be in the form of art, creative writing or poetry. Creative writing or poetry can be done on such topics as 'What the blind man would most like to see'.

2. Write a detailed job description for Jesus's job.

G 1. Lent 1

You will need:
A duster, a dustpan and brush

Introductory activity

Tell the children you are having a spring clean and you want everything clean and tidy. Ask some of them to dust and others to sweep. Ask them to pick up any litter they can see. (Plant some if your hall is tidy!)

Talk

In the spring people often have a spring clean. It is a chance to tidy everything up and throw away the rubbish that has collected.

Lent is about spring cleaning on the inside. It is easy to clean up the hall and make it look good but how do you clean up the inside of a person? How do you clean up thoughts and actions?

During Lent Christians ask God to help them clean themselves on the inside, to get rid of wrong thoughts and actions. Lent is the time before Easter (forty days, not counting Sundays) when Christians think carefully about themselves. They think about the things that need changing (cleaning) and they ask God's help for they believe that they cannot clean up on the inside without God's help.

Comment

Here is a bin and some paper. What sorts of things would Christians want to 'put in the bin'?
[Write on the pieces of paper some of the wrong things Christians try to clean up at Lent. Example: Telling lies.]
Just as we clear up rubbish and put it into a bin, so Christians try to clean out the rubbishy things in their lives during Lent.

Prayer

Thank you, Father, for the time of Lent when people can think about themselves and ask your help to change.

G 2. Lent 2

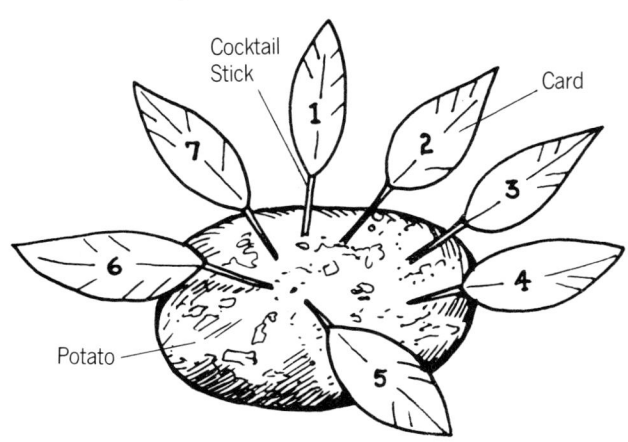

Cocktail Stick

Card

Potato

7 1 2 3 6 4 5

You will need:

A potato, paper (coloured or white), cocktail sticks, Sellotape, scissors, a pen.

Introductory activity

Draw a rough feather shape on the paper and cut out seven feathers. You can ask the children to help you with this.

Give each feather a number from one to seven.

Sellotape a cocktail stick to the back of each feather, leaving the point exposed.

Push all the feathers into the potato.

Talk

This is a Kukaras. In Greece children make these to use as calendars during Lent. During Advent some of you might have Advent Calendars. This is a Lenten Calendar. Lent is the time of year when Christians get themselves ready for Easter. They think about the things they have done and ask God to help them live better lives.

There are six Sundays in Lent. The children pull out one feather in the Kukaras on each Sunday of Lent. The last feather stands for Easter Day, when Lent is over.

Comment

For many people Christmas is an important festival, but for Christians Easter is the most important celebration. That is why children in many countries count down to Easter using a Lenten calendar.

Prayer

Thank you, Father, for the time of Lent when people look forward to Easter and try to get themselves ready.

G 3. Shrove Tuesday

SORRY PANCAKE

Letting people down

Not telling the truth

Not keeping a promise

You will need:
Paper, scissors, pens, a brown wax crayon, Blu-tak.

Introductory activity

Cut out a large pancake shape, as shown in the illustration. Rub over the pancake with the side of a brown wax crayon to give it a cooked effect.

Ask the children to suggest things people might say 'sorry' for. Write their suggestions in the pancake. Blu-tak the pancake to the wall.

Talk

Shrove Tuesday is the day before Lent starts. In this country we eat pancakes the day before Lent. In some other countries people have a big celebration on this day.

The word 'shrove' comes from the word 'shriven' which means 'to be forgiven'. On Shrove Tuesday people went to church and admitted what they had done wrong, the things they were sorry for, and asked God to forgive them. Shrove Tuesday could be called 'Sorry Tuesday' or 'Forgiveness Tuesday'.

Lent is a time when Christians think about Easter and they also think about themselves and the things which need changing. Just before Lent people used to eat pancakes to use up all their rich food because during Lent rich food and celebrations were not allowed. Today many Christians still give up something, such as chocolate, for Lent and donate the money they would have spent on it to charity.

Comment

Saying sorry is not easy. It is hard to admit you were in the wrong. However, saying you were wrong yesterday shows that you are a wiser person today.

Prayer

Thank you for the time of Lent, which is serious but also joyful as it looks forward to Easter and the day you rose again.

Holy Week – Teacher's Notes

Holy Week is the period between Palm Sunday and Easter Sunday. On each day a different event is remembered. These assemblies follow the pattern of Holy Week and there are also some separate assemblies which try to explain the significance of Easter for Christians.

G 4. Palm Sunday

You will need:
Paper, pens and Blu-tak.

Introductory activity

Ask the children how they greet each other (e.g. 'Hello', 'Hi' or, if you live in Nottinghamshire, 'Aye up, duck').

Here are some greetings from other countries:

Germany: Hallo, Willkommen.
France: Bonjour, Bienvenue.
Swahili: Jambo
Italian: Caiou

Ask the children if they know a greeting from any other language.

Story

When Jesus went into Jerusalem on the Sunday before the first Easter, he rode on a donkey, which was seen as an animal of peace. Crowds lined the streets and shouted 'Hosanna' and 'Welcome to God's special king'. They tore down branches from the trees and threw them on the ground for the donkey to walk on. Some took off their coats and threw them down to make a carpet.
　　The religious leaders were not pleased. 'Tell the crowd to shut up,' they said.
　　Jesus looked at them sadly. 'If I told the crowd to be quiet,' he said, 'the stones would start shouting instead.'

Comment

The crowds welcomed Jesus with the words 'Hosanna' or 'God Bless the King'. This was a very unusual welcome. Jesus's entry into Jerusalem is celebrated on Palm Sunday when Christians remember that they too welcome Jesus as their king.

Prayer

May we welcome you as the king, not as the king of a country, but as king of our lives and as prince of peace.

G 5. Monday – Cheating

You will need:
A small table to act as a stall and some items to sell.
Some toy money.

Introductory activity

Ask for volunteers to go shopping.

When you have all your shoppers ask them to buy items from the stall.

Once a couple of items have been bought, start cheating by giving the wrong change and refusing to give any more. Make it obvious that you are cheating.

Ask the rest of the children what you were doing wrong.

Story

Jesus went into the Temple to pray. As he went in he saw all the stalls in the courtyard selling animals and goods and changing ordinary money into special Temple money. Jesus noticed that many of the stall-holders were cheating and their main concern seemed to be making a profit. He was angry that the poor should be cheated of what little money they had. What made it worse was the fact that it was happening in God's house, a God of truth and honesty.

Jesus walked up to the money-changers and turned over their tables, scattering their money. He drove out the animals and the stall-holders with them. 'My Father's house should be a house of prayer,' he said. 'You have made it a den of robbers.'

Comment

Jesus turned out the cheating money-changers from the Temple because the Temple, like a church, is somewhere to pray and meet God, not a place for buying and selling, and particularly not for cheating. Jesus made it clear that God could not stand cheating or any type of dishonesty. Christians believe that truth, fairness and justice are very important.

Prayer

Thank you, God, that you are a God of truth and justice. Help us to copy you by being truthful and honest, fair and just.

G 6. Tuesday – Questions

Introductory activity

There are many different types of questions we can ask, such as:

What time is it?
Can I have a sweet?
What is 4 × 4?
Do you like playing rounders?

Ask the children for examples of different types of questions that they might ask.

Story

One day some people asked Jesus some questions. They asked questions to trick him, they asked hard questions and they asked silly questions. Jesus replied to all their questions carefully and did not fall for their tricks. The last question that Jesus was asked was a sensible one. A man asked Jesus what were the most important things in life. Jesus replied, 'Love God and love your neighbour.'

It is sometimes difficult to know who our neighbour is, but earlier on in his life Jesus had told a story to explain what he meant.

The story of the Good Samaritan

A man asked Jesus who his neighbour was and Jesus told him this story.

Once a Jewish man was travelling from Jerusalem to Jericho. The road went through a rough, stony area where robbers hid. As the man went along, robbers jumped out on him. They beat him up, stole all he had and left him half dead.

After a while another traveller came along, he was a priest from the Temple. When he saw the injured man he crossed over to the other side of the road to avoid him. Perhaps he was frightened, perhaps he thought that the robbers would attack him if he stayed around. We do not know. For some reason the priest left the injured man and did not help him. Later another man came by, he too worked in the Temple. When he saw the injured man he ignored him just as the priest had done. Perhaps he was busy or frightened or just did not want to be bothered. He too left the injured man lying in the road. Some time later a third man came along, he was a Samaritan. For a long time the Samaritans and the Jews had been enemies. But although the injured man was an enemy, the Samaritan stopped; he picked up the man, washed and bandaged his wounds, put him on his own donkey and took him to an inn. The Samaritan paid the owner of the inn to look after the injured man, and offered to pay any further expenses when he returned.

Comment

When Jesus had told this story, he asked the man who had questioned him which of the three had been the neighbour to the injured Jew. The man answered, 'The one who showed him kindness.

Today we use the word 'neighbour' to mean someone who lives next door, but for Jesus a neighbour was anyone, even the enemy.

Prayer

Help us to remember the two most important things in life – to love you and to love our neighbour.

G 7. Wednesday – Giving

You will need:
Some toy money and a money box or plate.

Introductory activity

Give five children different coins.

Ask the other children to say who has the most valuable coin and who has the least.

Ask a child to arrange the five pupils in order of the value of the coins they hold.

Now tell each of these children the amount they get for pocket money. You can write this on a piece of card if you wish and give to each child.

> The child with 1p gets 1p pocket money.
> The child with 5p gets 10p pocket money.
> The child with 10p gets 50p pocket money.
> The child with 50p gets £1 pocket money.
> The child with £1 gets £5 pocket money.

Ask each person to put their *coin* in the box/plate

Ask the other children to say who has given the most? Who would have the most pocket money left over if they had given that amount out of their pocket money?

Talk with the children about who has given the most. Was it the one who gave the highest value or the one who gave everything she had? Is it what we give that matters or what we have left over?

Story

The Poor Widow

One day when Jesus was in the Temple he saw people putting money in the collecting box. Many rich people went by and put in large amounts, then a poor widow came along and put in two small coins. Each coin was much less than a penny.

Jesus noticed the woman and said to his friends, 'That widow has put in more than all the rich people. They gave but still had lots left over, she gave everything she had.' *(Continued overleaf)*

Comment

On the Wednesday of Holy Week Christians remember the story of the poor widow who gave everything she had. Jesus recognized the immense gift this woman had given; she gave more than a millionaire could have given because she gave all she had. Christians believe that God does not count gifts by the amount of money a person puts in a box but by the amount they have left afterwards.

Prayer

Lord, help us to give unselfishly to those in need. Help us to give something valuable and not just our leftovers.

G 8. Thursday – The Servant King

Introductory activity

Talk with the children about kings and servants and their very different jobs. If you wish, you can wash another teacher's feet. Arrange this beforehand.

Story

The worst job for a servant in the time when Jesus lived was washing feet. In those days people wore sandals, the roads were dusty and it was very hot so people's feet got hot and sweaty. When a guest arrived at a house the servant would wash the guest's feet. Servants did not like this job so they used to give it to the youngest or least important servant to do.

When Jesus was with his disciples he wanted to talk to them about being humble, about not being boastful or proud. Instead of talking to them he took a bowl of water and a towel and washed their feet. Peter protested that Jesus shouldn't be doing such a dirty job. Jesus said that if he could do it, they should follow his example and never be too proud to do even the worst job for other people.

Comment

This event of washing the disciples' feet is remembered every year. The Pope still washes people's feet on the Thursday of Holy Week. Kings and queens used to wash the feet of the poor on Holy or Maundy Thursday, but now money is given instead. If you watch the news on Maundy Thursday you will see the Queen give special purses of money to elderly people. The purses contain the same number of coins as the monarch's age and she gives them to the same number of men and women as the number of years she has lived.

Prayer

Thank you, Father, for the example of Jesus who was prepared to do anything for other people and never felt that he was too important to do a dirty job.

G 9. Good Friday

NOTE: This is a difficult subject for young children to understand. Generally I would not advise raising such an issue in assembly when there is no time to follow up any repercussions with pastoral work. I have included an assembly on Good Friday, but approached it from the angle of sadness and avoided any *details* of the death. It is important that Good Friday is not separated from Easter Sunday or the children may be left thinking that this is the end of the story. Personally I prefer to deal with this subject in the classroom, but some teachers may like to have an assembly on Good Friday which staff can then follow up in class.

You will need:

A hot cross bun.
Card, pens and scissors.

Introductory activity

Ask the children what day it is and what the hot cross bun stands for.

Make a basic mask shape, as illustrated.

Talk to the children about how people look when they are sad. Gradually fill in the details of the mask to make it look sad, using suggestions from the children.

Talk

Good Friday is a very sad day for Christians. It used to be called God's Friday and it is the day when Christians remember Jesus's death. In many churches all the flowers are taken out, bright candlesticks and ornaments are covered and dark colours are used. People meet for worship and read the story of Jesus's death.

Comment

Although people are sad that Jesus died they remember that it is really GOOD Friday. Christians believe that Jesus's death defeated evil and made it possible for people to be close friends with God.

Christians also believe that Good Friday is only the beginning of the story; it is soon followed by Easter Sunday which celebrates Jesus coming alive again. Easter Sunday is so joyful it makes up for the sadness of Good Friday.

Prayer

Thank you, Father, that your son loved people enough to die for them. By wiping out the wrong of the past, he gave people a new start as friends of God.

G 10. Easter Saturday – Waiting

You will need:

An Easter garden, if possible, but this assembly can be done without it.

A simple Easter garden can be made using a tray with soil in. A cave is made by cutting a toilet roll centre in half and pushing it in the soil and placing a stone over the hole. A cross (or three crosses) can be placed in one corner of the garden (use two lolly sticks). Small flowers can be placed near the grave.

Introductory activity

Talk about the Easter garden, pointing out each part of it, or make the Easter garden in front of the children.

Alternatively, talk to the children about what it is like to wait for something.

Talk

Jesus's friends were very sad when he died. He was buried on the Friday and they waited all day Saturday because it was the Jewish sabbath – a holy day when they could not visit the grave. They wanted to go to the grave on the Sunday and take sweet-smelling flowers and herbs to put around Jesus's body, because they had not had time to do this on the Friday evening, before the sabbath started. It must have been hard to wait.

Comment

Christians have to wait on Easter Saturday. On Good Friday they remember Jesus's death, on Easter morning they celebrate Jesus's coming alive again, but on Easter Saturday they wait. Christians often have an Easter garden to remind them of the Easter story. On Good Friday they close the door to the tomb [show them the stone]. On Easter Sunday they open it up and show it is empty. On Easter Saturday they wait. Waiting is hard, but Christians know they are waiting for a really joyful day when they will celebrate Jesus coming alive again, which they call resurrection.

Prayer

Thank you, Father, that although we have to wait for Easter, we know we wait in certainty of a joyful celebration of the resurrection of Jesus.

G 11. Easter Sunday

You will need:
Scissors, pens and card.

Introductory activity

Using the basic mask shape, make a happy mask. Ask the children what a happy face looks like and fill in the details on the mask.

Story

Easter Sunday is the most joyful day in the year for Christians. The churches are full of yellow and white spring flowers, everything is bright and shiny and the worship is joyful. Christians read the story of the first Easter.

Here is part of the story they read.

Mary and the other women got up early to go to the tomb where Jesus had been buried. They took with them spices and sweet-smelling herbs to put on his body, for there had been no time to do this on the Friday when he was buried. As they walked along they wondered how they would roll away the enormous stone that was in front of the tomb. But when they arrived at the tomb they were amazed to find that it was already open and the guards had disappeared.

A man in white stood at the entrance and said to them, 'Why do you look for the living amongst the dead? He is not here any more, he is risen!' The women were afraid and ran back to tell the disciples.

Comment

This account of how the women discovered the empty tomb is only a part of the Easter story. Later on the disciples met the risen Jesus several times.

Easter is the most important time of the year for Christians. They believe that Jesus came alive again and defeated death. They are happy because he is still alive today and is their friend.

Prayer

Thank you, Father, that Jesus lives to be our friend.

G 12. The Meaning of Easter: Reconciliation

You will need:

Pritt Stick, Blu-tak, Sellotape, damaged toys (teddies with ears off, etc.), needle and cotton, a bandage.

Introductory activity

Show the children the damaged toys and ask for ideas about how to mend them. Ask them to select from the 'mending things' the right material to mend each item.

Try mending one or two with a piece of sellotape or glue.

Explain that it is not only toys that get broken, friendships get broken too. If a friendship is broken it is very hard to mend.

Bandage two children together by their thumbs, then ask if that makes them friends.

Asks the children for suggestions about mending friendships.

Story

The story of Joseph is about the mending of a broken friendship between some brothers.

Joseph was one of twelve brothers; he was one of the youngest. His father, Jacob, liked him more than his brothers, which was not fair. One day Jacob gave Joseph a special coat far better than anything his brothers had. This made Joseph's brothers very jealous. Why should their little brother be dressed better than they were? The more they thought about it the more jealous they became.

To make things worse, Joseph had some strange dreams. First he dreamt that all the sheaves of corn bowed down to him then he dreamt that the sun and the moon and eleven stars bowed down to him. Joseph realized that one day he would be an important person and many people including his own family would kneel to him. These dreams really annoyed his brothers and they decided that they could stand this spoiled child no longer. When they had Joseph alone they took off his new coat and dipped it in goat's blood and decided to tell their father that Joseph had been killed by a wild animal. They were going to leave Joseph to die down in a pit but instead they sold him as a slave to some Ishmaelites.

When Joseph arrived in Egypt he was sold to a man called Potiphar. Joseph worked very hard and became a valued servant until one day he was falsely accused of attacking Potiphar's wife and he was thrown into prison. For many years Joseph stayed in jail, frightened and alone.

One day two men joined him in prison. Both men had strange dreams which troubled them and Joseph told them what they meant. One of the men – a baker – was destined to be executed, but the other – a butler – was released and went back to work for the king or Pharoah. The butler promised to remember Joseph and try to help him, but he forgot all about him until one day when the king had two strange dreams.

The butler remembered that Joseph had helped him when he had had a puzzling dream. Joseph was called out of prison to unravel the king's nightmares. Joseph told the king that his strange dreams meant that there would be seven years of good harvest in Egypt and seven years of bad harvest. Joseph suggested they collect grain in the good years and store them ready for the bad years.

The seven years of good harvest and the seven years of bad harvest happened, just as Joseph had said. Instead of being sent back to prison Joseph was put in charge of collecting the food and became one of the most important men in Egypt.

When the seven bad years came, no one in Egypt went hungry, everyone had enough to eat. In Canaan, the land where Joseph's family lived, times were hard, they had very little to eat. Jacob sent his sons to Egypt to buy grain from the Egyptians. Joseph's brothers came to Egypt to buy food, but they did not recognize the little brother they had sold as a slave many years before.

Joseph wanted to be friends with his brothers again, but first he wanted to make sure they had changed. He asked a servant to plant a golden cup in one of the sacks of grain his brothers had brought. When the brothers were about to go, he called out 'Stop!' and accused them of stealing. Joseph went through all the sacks and found the golden cup in Benjamin's sack. The other brothers swore that Benjamin had not taken the cup, they protested that Benjamin was innocent. They offered to be slaves themselves rather than lose Benjamin. Joseph knew they were changed men and told them that he was their long-lost brother Joseph whom they had sold as a slave. Joseph forgave his brothers and invited them all to come and live in Egypt.

Comment

Joseph was willing to forgive his brothers but he wanted to make sure they had changed. Broken friendships can be mended only when one person forgives and the other person not only says sorry but really wants to change as well.

Forgiveness is the glue that mends broken friendships. Easter is all about forgiveness. Christians believe that God will forgive even the worst things that people do wrong. As Jesus was dying he asked God to forgive the people who hurt him. That does not mean that people can do what they like and then ask for forgiveness. Forgiveness means making a change; it means not wanting to do wrong any more.

Prayer

Thank you, Father, that you forgive us the wrong that we do and help us to change.

G 13. The Meaning of Easter: Jesus the Victor

You will need:
A rope.

Introductory activity

Talk about winning and losing.

Talk

In Jesus's time when the Roman army had a major victory they led their enemies captive behind them. That means they tied up the captives and led them through the streets whilst everybody cheered the winning soldiers.

[Loosely tie the rope around the hands of one child and show them how it was done.]

Sometimes the prisoners were tied behind the soldiers' chariots and people jeered at them as they passed.

Comment

Easter is about winning and losing. Christians believe it was a battle between good and evil, and good won. In the Bible Jesus is described as going on a victory march and leading his captives behind him, just like a Roman soldier, except that his enemies were not other soldiers but death and evil.

Prayer

Thank you, Father, that Jesus defeated evil and wrong, and now death is not the end of life but only the beginning.

G 14. The Meaning of Easter: New Life

You will need:
A dead plant and a live one.

Introductory activity

Look at the two plants and ask the children to notice the differences between them.

Story

Mary had been left in charge of the plants while her mother was away looking after a sick aunt. Mary was so busy playing that she forgot the plants until the day before her mum was due home. Mary looked at the plants, they were brown and withered. One was so limp that it almost bent over and touched the ground. The flowers had dropped off and the petals lay in shrivelled heaps in the pot and on the shelf. 'Maybe Mum won't notice,' she thought, but there was not much hope of that. It was Sunday and all the shops were closed so she could not replace the plants and anyway they would cost too much. Then Mary had an idea. She got some string and tied the plants to sticks which she pushed into the soil. That made them stand upright. Next she got her paint box and painted the brown leaves green again; they looked a bit odd but at least they were the right colour. She picked some flowers from the garden and glued them to the plants. With a bit of luck Mum would never notice . . . .

Comment

Do you think her Mum would notice? Why?

There is a great deal of difference between a dead plant and a live plant. Although you cannot see it, there is a lot of action going on inside a plant which results in leaves and flowers growing. Human beings are a bit like plants. Although you cannot see it, some people have a very live friendship with God which results in love and peace and joy. You can tell when someone has a live friendship with God just as you can tell when a plant is really alive. People with a live friendship with God should grow in love just as a live plant grows.

Easter is about new life – a life of friendship with God, a friendship that carries on beyond death.

Prayer

Thank you, Father, that we can grow in love as your friends. Thank you that death does not stop people being your friends, but that friendship carries on beyond death.

G 15. The Meaning of Easter: Remembering

You will need:
A diary.
A handkerchief with a knot in it.
A Remembrance Day poppy.
Any other aids to memory you can think of.

Set up a tray of six items for Kim's game.
Cover the items with a tea cloth.

Introductory activity

Ask the children how we remember things.

Show them your examples of memory aids.

Play Kim's game. Choose a child and ask her to remember all the items on the tray. Ask her to close her eyes while you remove one item and hide it under the cloth. Ask her what is missing.
Repeat this using other children.

Story

Just before he died, Jesus wanted to eat one last special meal with his friends. As he broke the bread so that he could share it with the others, he said, 'This is my body, broken for you.' As he poured out the wine, he said, 'This is my blood spilled for you. Whenever you eat bread and drink wine remember me and my body and blood.' The disciples did not really understand what he was talking about, but Jesus knew he was going to die and he was giving them a special way of remembering him.

Comment

Christians have a special 'meal' at which they eat a tiny piece of bread and take a small sip of wine to remind them that Jesus loved people enough to die for them. They also remember he is their special friend now. This meal has many different names; some Christians call it Communion, others call it Mass, The Breaking of Bread or Eucharist. Christians not only remember Jesus's death when they take Communion, they remember he is alive and close to them now.

Prayer

Jesus, we are thankful that when you had a goodbye meal with your friends it was not goodbye forever. We are thankful that you are still our friend now.

Follow-up Work for the Classroom

1. Make a Holy Week frieze. Cover a wall with frieze paper and divide it into seven sections. On each section mount children's writings and drawings that will explain what is remembered on that day. For Good Friday and Easter Sunday you can use the masks of sadness and joy.

2. Help the children to make an Easter garden.

3. With infants you might like to explore the subject of Easter using the book *Haffertees' First Easter* by J. and J. Perkins, published by Lion.